Handle with Care

Helping Children Prenatally Exposed to Drugs and Alcohol

Sylvia Fernandez Villarreal, MD
Lora-Ellen McKinney, PhD
Marcia Quackenbush, MS, MFCC

Suggestions for teachers, parents and other care providers of children to age 10

ETR ASSOCIA
Santa Cruz, Califo
1992

ETR Associates (Education, Training and Research) is a nonprofit organization committed to fostering the health, well-being and cultural diversity of individuals, families, schools and communities. The publishing program of ETR Associates provides books and materials that empower young people and adults with the skills to make positive health choices. We invite health professionals to learn more about our high-quality resources and our training and research programs by contacting us at P.O. Box 1830, Santa Cruz, CA 95061-1830.

 Published by ETR Associates, P.O. Box 1830, Santa Cruz, CA 95061-1830.

10 9 8 7 6 5 4

Printed in the United States of America

Illustrations by Marcia Quackenbush
Design by Ann Smiley and Julia Chiapella
Index by Nona Williams

Library of Congress Cataloging-in-Publication Data

Villarreal, Sylvia Fernandez.
Handle with Care : helping children prenatally exposed to drugs and alcohol / Sylvia Fernandez Villarreal, Lora-Ellen McKinney, Marcia Quackenbush.
p. cm.
"Suggestions for teachers, parents and other care providers of children to age 10."
Includes bibliographical references.
ISBN 1–56071–077–2
1. Children of narcotic addicts—United States. 2. Children of alcoholics—United States. 3. Child development—United States. 4. Infants—United States—Development. I. McKinney, Lora-Ellen. II. Quackenbush, Marcia. III. Title.
HV5824.C45V55 1992
362.29'23—dc20 91–37669

Title No. 594

Contents

Preface

We would like to dedicate this book to all children coping with prenatal chemical exposure, and to the caregivers who offer them love and hope for the future.

Over the past few years, we have been approached by many teachers and other providers who work with children. They have asked us for a resource offering information about children who have experienced prenatal exposure to drugs or alcohol—especially something that could help them understand the situation better, give them an idea of what they could do to respond, and help them build new skills.

We talked among ourselves about this idea, then spoke to others working with children exposed to drugs and alcohol. We were not aware of any resource that seemed quite right for these requests. Some focus solely on technical medical data without offering specific suggestions for front line providers. Others include great information, but are limited in scope. And we were aware that some of the new information being gathered on children with drug or alcohol exposure had not been tested extensively enough to make it to the pages of professional journals—providers had many personal experiences that were informative, but not yet published.

The idea for this book began to form. Based on what our colleagues told us, and what providers had asked for, we decided to write a book that included a general overview of the problem of prenatal substance exposure, described some of the common issues for children living in drug and alcohol involved families, and offered some practical suggestions for helping the children and their families. Additionally, we wanted very much to give providers a sense of hope in this work. The situation for children born drug or alcohol exposed is not a hopeless one, an important message we repeat throughout this book.

We also wanted to write something that would have useful information for a broad spectrum of providers working with children. As we reflected on the kinds of information to include here, we thought of teachers, counselors, medical providers, people working in community settings, volunteers and caregivers (parents or other primary support people). We have included a lot of material in this book for that reason.

As you look over the contents, you may find some sections are more relevant to your own interests than others, and we encourage you to "skip around" if that suits you. We think the book can work whether it is read straight through or in bits and pieces.

Maternal drug and alcohol use (the use of substances by a pregnant woman) is a problem that cuts across all class and ethnic lines. Cultural issues are especially significant in discussions about this subject. We are ourselves a multicultural team (Latina, African American and Anglo), and we put considerable emphasis during our planning and writing on producing a book that acknowledged and supported cultural differences.

We assume that if you are reading this book, it is because you work or advocate for children in some way. We take this opportunity to thank you for your dedication and hard work. We know the children in your life appreciate your efforts.

Acknowledgments

Many individuals offered us support, guidance and advice as we researched and developed this book, and others shared their personal stories and clinical experiences with us. Though as authors we take responsibility for errors or oversights in this book, its strengths must be shared with the wide array of dedicated providers who communicated their knowledge and wisdom to us very generously.

Special thanks go to Vickie Kropenske, Louise McKinney, Susan Kwok and Suzanne Giraudo for spending considerable time with us in interviews.

For reviewing manuscripts and providing feedback, we thank our friends and colleagues: Steven Batki, MD; Carol Cole; Donna Ferraro, MD; Amy Loulan; JoAnn Loulan; Louise McKinney; Anita Schriver; and Mary Alice Villarreal.

We would also like to thank our excellent editor, Kay Clark. She responded enthusiastically when we first approached her with our ideas for this book; she accommodated patiently as we adjusted content, chapter outlines and deadlines; she supported us through "blocks" and setbacks; and she even did some great editing once we finally had a manuscript for her.

Most of all, we thank the children we work with, who have provided us such an inspiring example of courage and perseverance in their excitement for learning and their enthusiasm for life.

Notes to the Reader

1. Interspersed between some of the chapters of this book are stories about children we have worked with. We hope these stories give you a sense of the broad range of experiences, strengths and challenges faced by children born to drug- or alcohol-involved parents. The profiles also illustrate the many solutions and hopeful outcomes possible when these children receive the attention of caring adults.

To protect confidentiality, the names and identifying information in our stories and case studies have been altered throughout this book. In some instances we have combined elements of different cases for purposes of illustration.

2. A glossary is included at the end of this book. To be clear about our meanings, you will want to be familiar with our definitions for a few especially important terms.

Provider: We use the term "provider" to refer to anyone providing service of some sort to children. This includes teachers, other educators, school administrators, counselors, social workers, physicians, nurses, church workers, childcare and day care staff, staff in community based organizations, volunteers working with children, and so on.

Caregiver: A child's primary support person may be a parent, foster parent, grandparent, aunt, uncle, cousin or adult sibling. We use the term "caregiver" to include anyone filling that special role in a child's life, whatever their biologic or legal relationship.

Children with prenatal chemical exposure: For our purposes, this term refers to children who have experienced prenatal exposure to drugs or alcohol because their mothers used such substances during pregnancy. We also use the terms "drug and alcohol exposure" and "substance exposure." We prefer this language to a term like "chemically exposed children" because it keeps the emphasis on the child rather than the symptom or condition.

Treatment and recovery: There are different theoretical approaches in programs that seek to help substance abusers stop using substances. A "treatment program," used most often in drug programs, is based on a medical model. A "recovery program," used most often in alcohol programs, is based on a spiritual and social model. We believe different kinds of programs will be effective for different individuals and in this book do not endorse one approach over the other.

Drug and alcohol involved families: Many children who have experienced prenatal substance exposure live in families where a parent or other member continues to use alcohol or drugs. Such families present many challenges, both for providers and for the children in the families. No discussion of the concerns of children with chemical exposure can be considered complete without addressing the issues of children living in drug- and alcohol-involved families.

Introduction

Few providers working with children today have not been alerted to the problem of prenatal drug and alcohol exposure. These are issues that have been with us for a long time, but they have become especially visible since the advent of the crack cocaine epidemic around 1985. We are familiar with the fact that children whose mothers used crack, alcohol or other substances during their pregnancies may have physical, social, emotional and academic problems.

The drug epidemic has presented us with problems of considerable dimension and scope. This is an epidemic that has affected educational, medical, social service, legal and legislative systems, requiring changed definitions of service and adjustments in policy. Children born drug or alcohol exposed may have to deal with many special challenges. But the situation is far from hopeless, and one of our major goals in writing this book is to persuade you of this fact.

Some children born to mothers who use drugs or alcohol will experience severe effects and significant impairment. Their problems may include intellectual, social, neurologic and learning difficulties. Their families may be utterly chaotic, unable to provide adequate care. These children will have limited capabilities and potentials.

Other children will be only mildly or moderately affected by their mothers' use of drugs or alcohol. They may socialize well with peers and adults, but have difficulty with some learning skills. They may be bright and capable of learning, but have limited impulse control, short attention spans or be easily frustrated. With special assistance, we can help children master these challenges and succeed in school and in social relationships.

Still other children will show no observable effects of prenatal chemical exposure. Only careful medical and developmental evaluation will be able to document irregularities in behavior or cognition related to early exposure to drugs or alcohol. The non-medical professional, without the use of specialized tools for assessment and evaluation, will be unable to detect any true difference between these children and others who have not experienced prenatal drug exposure.

There is no single "profile" that will describe the circumstances or needs of all children with prenatal chemical exposure. All of these children will benefit from stable home environments, appropriate schooling, consistency in care and relationships, and regular medical/developmental evaluation and follow-up. Some will require special attention in their school settings to help them compensate for differences in learning styles and information processing. A few—possibly only a very few—will require complete special education programs.

We should expect the majority of children born to substance-using mothers to be integrated into regular education classes and to be active members of community-based children's programs. The teaching techniques for working with these children in the regular classroom are not new to teachers. In most cases, longstanding and well-tried academic and behavior management approaches will be most useful. For most children with chemical exposure, teachers will be able to create an appropriate learning environment with only moderate adjustment in classroom design and routine. Similar techniques will be helpful for those working with children in non-school settings.

Many children with chemical exposure will face significant challenges in their lives, and we acknowledge that their needs place some additional burdens on schools and communities. Often the greatest effort, however, is made by the children themselves, along with the members of their extended families—their mothers, fathers, grandparents, aunts and uncles, godparents, cousins and older siblings.

These children are great fighters, overcoming tremendous odds in the newborn period and surviving through perseverance and wit as they grow.

Most of the families are deeply devoted to their children, and are eager for understanding and assistance.

This book is meant to serve as a guide to help providers who work with children—including teachers, workers in recreation programs and churches, health care workers and people involved in community programs—join in a collaborative effort to help children with drug or alcohol exposure and their families.

What Can Providers Learn from This Book?

This book offers useful information and practical suggestions for front-line providers working with children. Though different providers may need different kinds of information about children with drug and alcohol exposure, we all share common goals. We want to help children be physically healthy; we want them to have loving attachments to family and friends; and we want them to succeed in their schools and their communities.

In this book, we have included information we think will be useful to teachers, health care workers, staff in community projects, counselors and case managers, and parents or other caregivers. The relevance of each section of the book may vary depending on your own role with children, but we believe the comprehensive picture presented by the book overall will be helpful too.

If you are a worker at an early childhood day care center, you may find the information in Chapter 7 especially helpful. From this, you can learn how to hold, feed or diaper a child with prenatal chemical exposure. If you are an elementary school teacher, this chapter can provide background on the early experiences of some of your students.

School teachers will find suggestions for classroom applications in Chapters 8 and 9. A youth group leader might use some of these suggestions in planning activities. And, after reading these chapters, a caregiver may understand more about ways a school can help his or her child learn and will be better prepared to advocate for a more appropriate educational plan.

The importance of educating ourselves about the issues faced by children living in drug- or alcohol-involved families cannot be overemphasized. The scope of the problem is broad and affects children of all ethnic and socioeconomic backgrounds. Anyone who works with children in this country today will be working with children who have experienced prenatal chemical exposure and with children who live in families affected by chemical dependency.

Providers have an extraordinary opportunity to help such children maximize their potential, find worth in lives that are often difficult, and contribute meaningfully to the communities that nurture them. In our role of providing support and encouragement to the families and the children, we may be offering the greatest help of all—pride in the accomplishments of the present and hope for the possibilities of the future.

Chapter 1

Prenatal Drug and Alcohol Exposure: What's Really Going On?

When a pregnant woman uses substances such as alcohol, nicotine, prescription or recreational drugs, the substances pass through the placenta, affecting her fetus as well. The emphasis of this book is on the children of women who have actual chemical dependencies—that is, they are using a substance addictively. But it is important to remember that even small amounts of drugs or alcohol can impair fetal development, and a single episode of use very early in the pregnancy may be quite dangerous for the fetus.

One way we can begin to understand the scope of this problem is to look at how widespread maternal substance use is. How many pregnant women, or women of childbearing age, are actually using drugs or alcohol? How many children are born suffering some effects of prenatal substance exposure?

The Trouble with Measuring the Problem

Unfortunately, efforts to survey pregnant women, new mothers and infants present problems and do not give us the precise information we would like. There are three standard methods for measuring prenatal drug and alcohol exposure: (1) self-report of substance use by pregnant women or new mothers; (2) toxicology screening of a woman's urine or blood during pregnancy; and (3) toxicology screening of a newborn's urine soon after birth.

Self-report surveys of drug or alcohol use are problematic in any population. Under-reporting is a typical bias of the results, and often it is considerable. For example, one study showed that of women who tested positive on toxicology screens at labor and delivery, only 27 percent had self-reported use of substances when asked (Miller, 1989).

Toxicology screening of mother or infant is another strategy for measuring maternal substance use. It is standard practice in hospital settings to carry out a toxicology screen if a woman admits to drug use during the pregnancy or at the time of labor and delivery. In most cases, a woman must give consent for such screening. If mother or infant shows signs or symptoms of drug use at delivery, a toxicology screen can also be done on the newborn. This screen can be completed without the mother's consent if necessary.

Habitual users of drugs are typically very skilled at hiding their use, however. Even a trained clinician may be unable to identify drug users.

In general, private insurance patients are suspected of drug use less often than uninsured or public fund patients, and providers to the middle and upper class are less willing to act on suspicions of drug use. One study showed that while levels of marijuana and cocaine use in a maternal population were virtually identical across economic and ethnic lines, Black women were ten times more likely to be reported to health authorities for substance use than White women, and poor women were more likely to be reported than affluent women (Chasnoff, Landress and Barett, 1990).

Even when they are performed, toxicology screens are not entirely reliable measures. Most substances can only be measured in the urine or blood for a short period after use—24 hours to a few days. Unless screens are done frequently and regularly throughout the pregnancy, intermittent users can easily be missed. Some of the tests have a high false negative rate, so even a woman who actively uses during the time of screening may have a negative result on her test.

In the newborn, screens of urine can also be inaccurate or confounding. If the mother has not used substances within 24 hours of delivery, the screen may be negative. Some women who use drugs delay going to the hospital at the time of labor to diminish the chances of a positive toxicology screen being taken. False-negatives are also a problem with newborn screens. In one case, a woman had twins who were screened—one was positive for cocaine, the other was positive for PCP (phencycladine) only.

In 1989, the National Association for Perinatal Addiction Research and Education (NAPARE) reported on a survey that sought to determine the number of infants born after prenatal exposure to illegal drugs. They examined a total of 300 births from 36 hospitals nationwide, both private and public, encompassing all economic groups. They found that 11 percent of the mothers had used illegal drugs during pregnancy.

These findings suggest that as many as 375,000 children are being born *annually* in the United States with prenatal drug exposure. The survey results do not include the estimated 40,000 children born annually with some form of alcohol-related birth defect, or thousands more whose mothers smoked cigarettes or used prescription drugs during pregnancy.

The NAPARE study involved hospitals in metropolitan areas, and some researchers have suggested that results from hospitals in rural or suburban areas would be lower. But surveys in suburban and rural areas suggest that drug use and prenatal drug exposure are on the rise throughout the country, and surveys of suburban hospitals have shown three- to four-fold increases in the number of infants born drug exposed since 1985. Prenatal drug and alcohol exposure is not solely a problem of inner cities.

Often, providers who attempt to gather statistics on drug and alcohol exposure of infants charge that researchers' estimates are consistently low. Providers' own experience suggests that prenatal substance exposure is a much more widespread phenomenon than research estimates indicate.

> "Whenever I look at statistical reports about drug use by pregnant women, I feel like I'm wearing some special kaleidoscopic glasses that can change the appearance of the picture. If you manipulate the statistics one way, it looks like just about everybody in the world is using dangerous substances during pregnancy. If you turn them another way, it doesn't look like much of a problem at all. In my clinic, whether the rate is 2 percent or 25 percent isn't really very important to me. The problem is there, the kids are being affected, and we really need to try to help them and their families."
>
> —Pediatric nurse practitioner

Why Do Pregnant Women Use Drugs?

Pregnant women use drugs for the same reasons that men or other women do. When a substance enters the body, the euphoria or other pleasant sensations may be very powerful. A person wants to use the substance again. When the substance begins to leave the body, the withdrawal effects may be very unpleasant. The person wants to avoid this discomfort. Use of drugs or alcohol is an easier choice, in the short term, and feels much better.

Ideally, a pregnancy is a wonderful and mysterious thing. A new life is developing—a symbol of hope, renewal and the promise of the future. A unique physical bond exists between the mother and her fetus. She has a remarkable opportunity to protect this vulnerable being, nourish it and provide it a safe environment in which to grow.

For many pregnant women, however, the reality is far from ideal. The pregnancy may be unplanned or unwanted. Early on, especially in the case of teenagers and young women, the woman may not even realize she is pregnant. Some women live in abusive relationships; others are burdened by family problems and demands. They may be struggling to care for other children. They may be undereducated, unemployed and living in poverty or on the edge of it. They may suffer from depression, low self-esteem and a limited sense of self-efficacy.

When women in these circumstances develop chemical dependencies or drug problems, they are less likely to seek treatment and recovery services. (See Chapter 4 for more information.) Most women who use drugs or alcohol during a pregnancy have well-established addictions before they become pregnant.

Substance use is influenced by personality, social factors, environment and, most importantly, peers. Reasons for using are as varied as users themselves, but ultimately come down to one thing at the outset: the person believes the substance will make him or her feel better in some way—higher, more relaxed, more popular, more accepted, safer, sexier, more grown-up, more rebellious, stronger.

Elena, 18 years old, has gone to a big party with her friend Rosa. They know some of the people there, and there are a lot of new people too. They both have a couple of drinks to relax and make it easier to socialize. A young man named Hector introduces himself and offers them a hit from his crack pipe.

Elena hesitates. She has never used crack before and has heard it is a dangerous drug. But Rosa chides her. "Come on, relax. It's fun! You won't get addicted. Don't worry." Rosa takes the first hit. Elena doesn't want to be left out, and Rosa looks like she really enjoys the crack. So Elena takes a few hits too, with the help of Hector's friendly instruction.

Elena does enjoy the crack, and Hector shares his pipe with her several more times that evening. She feels strong and secure and safe when she uses the pipe. She has no idea that she is three weeks pregnant.

Most people try a substance because they have heard it will make them feel different in some way. If the substance does create a pleasant sensation (or if the user believes it does), future use is reinforced. It often seems to a user that individual incidents of use in safe settings will not be dangerous.

In reality, of course, there are many instances where potential dangers do exist. Drugs and alcohol can adversely affect a person's ability to drive an automobile, operate heavy machinery, or pay attention at school or work. Users often combine drugs, or use drugs with alcohol or prescription medications, and these combinations can create dangerous and sometimes fatal physical reactions.

There may be unexpected consequences to drug use. A person might have an allergic reaction, go into heart failure or respiratory arrest, or inadvertently overdose on a drug. And, as we have mentioned, if a woman is pregnant, use of drugs or alcohol can affect the health of her fetus. Illicit drugs by definition are marketed illegally, and without manufacturing and marketing controls, users cannot know with certainty what they are getting when they buy illegal drugs.

These acute effects of drug use pose genuine dangers for users. Of equal or greater concern is the potential for an individual user to develop a chemical dependency and engage in chronic use of a substance.

Chemical Dependency and Chronic Drug Use

Most individuals who develop dependencies deny the problem for a long time. By the time they actually recognize they have a problem (if ever), they are usually unable to stop using without outside help. With continued use, the health effects become much more dangerous, the psychological and emotional consequences greater, and the financial and social burdens more profound. In the grip of a serious dependency or physical addiction, a user may sacrifice virtually anything necessary to get his or her substance.

> "I stole my best friend's camera and sold it to buy heroin. I was there in her house, and her camera was just sitting out on the dresser, and I knew she would never notice me taking it. I felt terrible about it, but—hey—I was a junkie. Nothing was more important than getting my heroin for the day."
>
> —Former heroin addict

Chemical substances can have physical, neurologic, emotional, behavioral and social effects. Some substances create physical dependence, and a sudden cessation of use can lead to life-threatening withdrawal effects. This is true for alcohol, heroin and Valium, for example.

Other substances create psychological dependence, meaning a person will not die or suffer serious physical health consequences if use of the drug is suddenly stopped, but will feel extreme discomfort and a strong craving for the substance. This is the case with marijuana and cocaine.

Drugs that create psychological dependence are not less dangerous than those that lead to physical dependence. The potential dangers of any addictive substance are considerable, and the user's life, whatever the substance of choice, will be affected in many different areas. (See Appendix A for background information on a number of commonly abused substances.)

Like other addicted individuals, chemically dependent pregnant women are driven by their dependencies. They may want to protect their own health, the health of their fetuses, the well-being of their families and the integrity of their relationships. But in the face of a true dependency or addiction, this becomes virtually impossible. Pregnant women who use dangerous substances are not deliberately trying to harm their fetuses. In many cases they are aware of the dangers their use poses to the fetus. They are simply unable to stop using. Even women who are highly motivated to stop will usually not be successful without the assistance of competent treatment and recovery programs, and few such programs exist.

How Substances Affect the Fetus

When a pregnant woman uses a chemical substance, the substance crosses the placental barrier and enters the fetal bloodstream. The effects of this transplacental crossing can be mild and transient; for example, a fetus's physiology may be accelerated or depressed for a short period of time. However, depending on the substance, the frequency of maternal use and the stage of fetal development at the time of use, effects can also be severe and long lasting.

The specific effects of drug exposure will vary among different substances, but some of the common manifestations during pregnancy and birth include poor nutrition, risk of infections and problems in delivery. The newborn may suffer slow growth and small size, immaturity in the lungs, prematurity, newborn drug withdrawal, seizures, irritability, feeding problems, brain damage, developmental delay, malformations of major organs (heart, kidney, brain), and sudden infant death syndrome (SIDS).

The costs of caring for moderately to severely affected newborns is considerable, and the children face potential medical and developmental problems in the future. (See Appendix B for information about the effects of common substances on pregnancy, birth outcome and fetal and child development.)

How Substances Affect Children as They Grow

Some children have social difficulties as they grow and mature. They may be more self-centered and aggressive than other children, more withdrawn and timid, or just seem unable to "connect" with adults or other children. Others have behavioral problems—impulsivity and aggressiveness, emotional lability (fast-changing emotional states), hostility or depression. Some have learning problems, such as short attention spans or differences in how they perceive and process information. (See Chapter 6 for more detailed information about the effects of chemical exposure on fetuses and newborns.)

Many reports have linked these medical, developmental, social and learning difficulties to prenatal exposure to drugs or alcohol. Substances do pose specific and significant risks to fetuses. However, it is not always possible to determine a cause/effect relationship in a particular child. It is difficult for researchers to separate all the various influences that may negatively affect a child's physical, cognitive and social development.

If a child is delayed in reaching developmental milestones, is that delay caused by a particular prenatal chemical exposure? poverty or family violence? poor nutrition? parental neglect or abuse? multiple placements in foster homes? chronic illness? long hospitalizations? family difficulties related to the special demands of the neonatal period?

Any combination of these factors may be present in the life of a child with prenatal chemical exposure, and all are likely to influence the child's development.

Some children who have experienced prenatal chemical exposure are likely to need careful individual evaluation and assessment. Ideally, the family will be evaluated along with the child. Interventions can be planned involving medical care, family counseling and support, educational assistance and involvement in special developmental enrichment programs.

These interventions must be recommended based on the individual child's particular strengths and needs, not based solely on a known or suspected history of drug or alcohol exposure. More detailed information on these issues is included in later chapters.

Despite the difficulty of gathering precise statistics on prenatal drug and alcohol exposure, it is clear the scope of of the problem is broad. The effects on individual children, their families and their communities are considerable. The financial costs are high. Drug and alcohol exposed infants often require expensive hospital care for weeks after birth, and severely affected children will continue to need special medical care.

Children with moderate to severe effects of chemical exposure will often require full or partial special education programs. Community programs already overburdened by tightening budgets and increasing demands must struggle to adjust existing programs, or create new ones, to respond to the needs of children with drug and alcohol exposure and their families.

What We Can Do

There *are* things we can do. We can offer interventions that acknowledge and support the importance of the family to the children's well-being. We can help children develop strengths and skills to cope with any hardships they might face. We can remember that individual children deserve careful evaluation and assessment, and that each child's needs will be somewhat different from his or her peers.

For example, imagine you are a school teacher and you have a student you know is living in an alcoholic home. You can make a special effort to reach this student with messages about self-worth and positive self-esteem, areas that are quite damaged for a child with an alcoholic parent.

Or you teach a Sunday school class with a number of children whose parents use or formerly used drugs or alcohol. Some of the children have short attention spans and are quite noisy. Others seem quiet and withdrawn. You probably don't know whether these are effects of prenatal chemical exposure, but you can still plan your classes using the principles described in Chapter 9.

Or perhaps you are a counselor at a day camp for young children and a child in your program is clumsy and awkward and has trouble with hand-eye coordination. You see his mother, whom you know to be a former drug user, criticizing him because he can't catch a ball. Maybe the child's clumsiness is caused by prenatal drug exposure, maybe not. But you can share with the mother some of the success you have had with the boy by using larger balls, slow movements, and positive reinforcement for his efforts.

In none of these instances is the child's problem "solved." In none of them is there a sudden, dramatic change for the better. But small steps on the part of caring providers will have helped each child cope a little better.

Offering personal and genuine attention to children and their families, even in a small way, can have a true impact on the overall quality of their lives. Using the suggestions in this book and your own good sense about children and their families, we believe you can have an effect that will influence such situations positively.

Chapter 2

Understanding Cultural Issues: Helping You Help Children

The problems of children with chemical exposure, along with the related problems of family drug and alcohol use, are significantly influenced by a variety of factors we call "cultural issues." Many people consider culture primarily a matter of race, or perhaps a manifestation of ethnicity, but we are defining culture in much broader terms.

For our purposes here, we define culture as a common way that members of a group see things in the world. This includes the group's assumptions about the world, other people, right and wrong, good and bad, important and not important. It also includes the group's codes of behavior—what behaviors are acceptable under what circumstances.*

An individual's vision of the world, and of acceptable behavior, can be strongly reinforced by a shared group experience. For example, if a classroom of African American schoolchildren hears a dynamic speaker talk about Black pride and the extensive cultural accomplishments of African societies, the children may feel more positive about themselves individually and as a group. They may begin to speak openly of this pride, and to integrate knowledge about African history into their play. The children might even play at being African warriors at one point, rather than cowboys.

Similarly, a drinker who needs to get home after having a half dozen gin and tonics at the local bar, may feel apprehensive about driving. After discussing the matter with other drinkers, who have a considerable investment in denying the problems associated with drinking, however, he or she may be encouraged to "just take it easy" and drive on home. In the culture of drinkers, there is a shared belief that many people aren't really affected by alcohol, and that such individuals are entirely justified driving, even after six drinks.

Being aware of some of the cultural issues in the substance use arena can help us achieve a more compassionate understanding of the demands faced by drug-involved families and a better sense of the family environment in which the children live. This awareness can help us plan effective strategies for communicating with parents and caregivers about their children. And we can gain a more realistic sense of our own role, whatever it may be, in the struggle to cope with the problems of children with chemical exposure.

* This definition is based substantially on a definition of culture by Noel Day, Executive Director, Polaris Research and Development, San Francisco, California.

A teacher, for example, may be perceived by drug-involved parents in a poor neighborhood as being too "different" (middle class, well-educated, without serious problems) to understand the demands faced by their family. The teacher will be more effective with parents if he or she can communicate in some way, subtly or directly, a realistic sense of what the children's lives are like, without being critical of the parents or the community.

A counselor working with a child from an educated, middle class family may come across parents who deny that the father's use of cocaine and marijuana is harmful to the child in any way. The counselor can offer evidence that parental substance use and addiction is indeed harmful for children, perhaps using examples from books, popular parenting authorities or statistical reports. If the parents are even partially convinced, the counselor may be able to continue providing support to the child. The father might even be persuaded to see a substance abuse specialist to assess his use.

Regions, Communities and Neighborhoods

All regions, and subcommunities within each region, have their own "cultures" of substance use. The cultures determine what substances are popular, how they are ingested, and, to some extent, how frequently they are used. We also see regional and neighborhood differences in the street terminology for drugs, users' beliefs about the effects of drugs, and users' understanding of the risks of a particular drug. A drug that is acceptable in one community may be considered dangerous, unpleasant or just "not hip" in another. The social rules for the purchase and use of drugs may also vary by region.

In some populations, alcohol is the substance of choice; in others, it might be crack cocaine or PCP. In one community, users of cocaine may ingest the drug primarily through smokable crack, while in another, users snort powdered cocaine or prepare solutions for intravenous injections.

A particular drug combination may become especially popular for a period of time. Social settings for use also vary. For example, "shooting galleries" (where injection drug users can go to rent a syringe and buy a fix) are considerably more widespread in New York City than in Los Angeles or

Chicago. As times and trends change, so do the drugs of choice and the methods of their use.

Knowing what's going on in the local community can help you understand more about what's going on in the homes of the children with whom you work. If you are an elementary school teacher working in a neighborhood where crack cocaine is very popular, for example, you can probably assume that most of your students have seen crack being used, that some see it used regularly in their homes, and that many will respond emotionally to the prevalence of crack use by demonstrating academic or behavioral difficulties.

You might anticipate certain problems among your students, and in response offer the children opportunities to discuss how to cope with family difficulties or how to maintain a sense of personal pride and dignity in the face of family problems.

It is also useful to become familiar with resources for families coping with chemical dependency. If you are a recreation director in a neighborhood children's program and you learn that one of the children's parents is using drugs, knowing local trends in drug use might suggest what substance the parent is using. Ideally, you would know of a local program that has had success helping drug-involved families. The ability to demonstrate understanding of the problem, acceptance of the parent, and concern for the well-being of child and family may allow you to suggest in a non-threatening way that the parent seek treatment.

Ethnic Trends and Traditions

Often, trends in substance use can be discerned along ethnic lines as well. This information may be useful in suggesting overall strategies for planning prevention and establishing treatment programs.

For example, if there is a high rate of alcoholism among an urban Native American community, prevention programs might consider distributing print and media materials that use Indian cultural images or concepts. The health department might hire Native American outreach workers to educate users about treatment options, and the treatment community might establish a detoxification program that integrates Native American cultural values and language capabilities.

Attitudes about substances vary by culture, and knowing a family's cultural belief about drugs or alcohol may help a provider offer more useful guidance or intervention.

In some traditional Latino families, for example, drug use is frowned upon in general, but accepted among men as long as the man is also able to care for "la familia," the family. He must be able to provide food and clothing for the children, keep a roof over their heads, and purchase books necessary for their schooling. If you are a drug counselor working with a Latino man from such a family, you might emphasize the importance of this role and explore whether he has been able to meet his family obligations.

Individuals do not always abide by the trends of their ethnic culture, of course. We cannot make assumptions about a person based solely on his or her ethnic affiliation. As always, in the area of substance abuse and drug-involved families, individual assessment is essential.

Economic Influences

Trends in drug use are also influenced by a community's economic status. The crack cocaine epidemic has reached extraordinary growth largely for economic reasons. Before this inexpensive drug appeared on the market, it was difficult to get into the business of dealing—one needed a capital outlay of several hundred dollars to deal a drug like marijuana, and tens of thousands to deal cocaine or heroin. Additionally, many of these markets were strictly controlled by organized crime or gangs.

But anyone with fifty dollars can buy and resell crack cocaine at a profit. With an investment of a few hundred dollars, someone using rudimentary skills and equipment can be selling a personal "brand" of crack in a short period of time.

Teenage youths, mostly male, have found an easy, profitable (and dangerous) niche running and dealing crack cocaine. Large numbers of people, even people who are quite poor, can afford to buy the rocks. The market demand for this bargain drug is high, production is cheap and easy, and manufacture and dealing of crack cocaine is widespread.

Women and Drugs

Women of childbearing age and pregnant women are more likely than men to live in poverty and be responsible for dependent children. This combination of circumstances presents women with certain difficulties in accessing health care, drug treatment programs, education or other services.

Women are often unable to pay for fee-based services. Even for free or low-cost programs, transportation becomes a problem. A woman may not own a car, be able to afford the bus or cab fare, feel capable of managing several children on public transportation, or be able to arrange and afford childcare.

Many women who use drugs, therefore, are unable for practical reasons to seek help for treatment and recovery. There is also a shortage of spaces for women, especially pregnant women or women with children, in treatment and recovery programs. (See Chapter 4 for more information.)

Women with limited income and transportation options are likely to use the cheapest drug easily available in the neighborhood. In a considerable number of cases, this will be alcohol and/or crack cocaine.

Women are also more likely than men to experience clinical depression. Because they may be unable to afford or seek treatment for depression, many will use whatever substance is readily available to get relief. Chemical dependency can be easily established for a woman with untreated depression or other mental health problems.

The complex problems of dual diagnosis—psychiatric illness coupled with chemical dependency—place significant demands on providers trained to deal with only one half of the problem. Few programs can help individuals who have both a psychiatric and a substance use problem.

Women also have more difficulty with low self-esteem and tend to have a lower sense of self-efficacy then men. They may see few personal alternatives for the future, little hope that their lives will improve, and no respite from their troubles other than the escape provided by drug or alcohol use. Their depression grows, in part, from the hopelessness of their situation.

There is some evidence that women metabolize alcohol differently than men because of the higher fat content in their bodies. They become intoxicated with less liquor, and may become addicted to alcohol or other drugs more quickly than men.

Women are also more likely than men to be solitary drinkers or users—they use their substances alone at home because they have to stay with their children, or they have no car, or it is dangerous for them to go out at night. Alcoholism and addiction in women are often under-recognized and under-reported because of the more secretive nature of their use.

Gender also appears to influence choice of drugs. Although there are many women who use injection drugs, women in general are more attracted to drugs that can be swallowed (alcohol, pills) and smoked (marijuana, crack cocaine) than those that must be injected. New, cheap forms of smokable methamphetamines ("ice") and heroin are appearing on the market now, on the heels of the crack epidemic. Women will be especially susceptible to new drugs of this nature.

Women who are chemically dependent, but do not have money to buy their substance, may trade sex for drugs. Reports of this have become widespread since the advent of the crack epidemic, and the trading of sex for crack is especially common.

This is not a new behavior. Women have traded sex for alcohol or drugs for centuries. It does raise the additional health risk of sexually transmitted diseases, including HIV/AIDS; the risk of battery and rape; and the risk of becoming pregnant during a period of addictive drug use.

The Drug Culture: A Special Concern

One of the most insidious effects of chemical dependency is the increasing involvement of users in the drug culture. They like being around others who use, they want to talk about the drug, they become obsessed with their substance, and they need to make connections with people who can keep them supplied. They enjoy using in an atmosphere of acceptance—in a place where everyone's use is addictive, they are less likely to feel they have a problem.

The culture of drug use and dealing does more than provide an aura of acceptability for the chemically dependent person, however. Once the attachment to the drug culture is made, the individual runs the risk of becoming acclimated to other aspects of this culture as well.

The drug culture places a low value on human life. Dealers may cut their product with a variety of dangerous materials, including talcum powder (which can cause embolisms if injected), benzocaine, PCP (phencycladine), quinine, methamphetamines and strychnine.

Users may endanger the well-being of friends, family, other users or complete strangers in their efforts to obtain their drug, to obtain money to buy their drug, or as a consequence of being under the influence. This disregard for human life has become especially extreme within the crack trade, where shootings related to turf wars commonly end in the death of neighbors, including young children, completely uninvolved in drug use or transactions.

The drug culture also institutionalizes the degradation of women, sometimes to an extraordinary degree. Stories abound among drug providers of ways women have been humiliated, raped or beaten by drug-involved men. A woman's dependence on a man to supply her with drugs may leave her with little self-respect.

The welfare of children is of little concern in the drug culture. Users are encouraged to build increasing dependencies and spend more money on drugs and less on their families. Chronic use of alcohol or drugs often leads to family violence, and the incidence of physical and sexual abuse is higher in families with a chemically dependent parent.

Increased rates of neighborhood crime and violence related to drug use and trade jeopardize children's lives. Children at increasingly young ages are being used as runners or put on watch for police. Youth gangs are glamorized, and children in early elementary grades sometimes join the gangs as "mascots."

As users become more dependent on their substance, they may take on more of the values of the drug culture. The values of their culture of origin become more foreign and more difficult to reconcile with the standards of the drug culture. They may lose contact with their extended families, abuse or neglect their children, or give up the spiritual beliefs of their youth. They often find it increasingly difficult to acknowledge feelings of love, sadness, fear or anger, and cease to care about anything as much as they care about their substance.

The Family as a Key to Recovery

In working with children who have experienced prenatal exposure to drugs or alcohol, the emphasis on the family is especially important because the family is the single most important influence in the child's life. We will have limited success with children if we do not also intervene in effective ways with their families.

Chemical dependency is a family disease. (See Chapter 5 for further information.) If the family is not involved in treatment, family members will typically "enable" the chemically dependent person—that is, they will support continued use of the substance, often in an unconscious or covert fashion.

Often, drug-involved families distrust providers. They may fear that efforts to help are actually aimed at breaking up the family. These fears are not entirely unfounded—a teacher, counselor or health care worker who suspects child abuse or neglect is obligated to report this to the authorities. The families know this and will often give misleading information to providers or avoid contact with schools or service agencies.

Chemically dependent parents often have low self-esteem and lack experience in childcare. Some are teen mothers who are themselves children of teen mothers. There may be no one in the extended family who is actually confident and knowledgeable about the proper care of children.

The child with substance exposure often has special needs, and may have complicated requirements for medical care. Young mothers and chemically dependent mothers are often needy themselves, and, while they care about their children deeply, they may also feel jealous of the attention the child receives. Or they may fear the child will become more attached to a provider than to them and sabotage the relationship in some way.

Families learn how to operate in relationship to their culture. The expectations and obligations of family members may be culturally determined. The family may be the place an individual expects to find nurturing and understanding or structure and discipline. Children may be expected to show great respect for and total obedience to elders.

Individual children and adults may have considerable responsibility for the well-being of younger family members. The needs of the individual may be less important than those of the family unit. A mother or father, or perhaps a grandparent or great aunt, may be the figurehead of the family, the one who makes the significant decisions, the one who can influence the individuals and the family as a whole.

Understanding the cultural beliefs of a drug-involved family will help people who work with the children. For example, you may be more successful in some instances by showing respectful deference to the head of the family, and in other situations by acting with firm but loving authority.

Parents and other family members need constant reinforcement that their role is essential, of great importance to the child, and cannot be duplicated by a provider who is not part of the child's family. You must emphasize that your role is to support the family's place of importance in the child's life. The ability to intervene to help the child in a way that is consonant with the family's values will increase the likelihood of success.

Prevention, Treatment and Culture

Most children with drug and alcohol exposure live with parents, grandparents or other relatives, and the dynamics of chemical dependency may continue to affect the children and their families. Drug abuse prevention will be essential for children from drug involved families, and prevention and treatment opportunities should be available for families as well.

Cultural differences influence success rates in treatment and recovery efforts. Different interventions seem to be effective to different degrees for different cultures. Alcoholics Anonymous, Narcotics Anonymous and other 12-step programs have, thus far, been most successful with middle and working class people. Community-based programs and church programs have had success working with transient, homeless and poor populations.

Some excellent programs have been established through African American churches which specifically serve the African American community. Gay community agencies have provided programs for lesbian and gay youth who have felt unwelcome, or even been refused admittance, at other programs. Extended families and Catholic priests have been successfully involved in programs serving the Latino community in some cases.

Many of these approaches reflect differences in the cultural beliefs of a community. How is the family defined, and who is included? How much trust is placed in authority? How are members of other cultures viewed? How serious is the problem of substance abuse within the cultural community? What is the individual's perceived role in controlling life events? How important are the individual's needs compared to the family's needs?

Traditional treatment approaches are often very directive and sometimes very individually oriented. Twelve-step programs use a philosophy of "powerlessness" to help participants develop a sense of relationship with a higher power that can support them in maintaining sobriety.

This directive approach may inhibit some individuals from developing their own sense of personal commitment to recovery. They may either comply with or rebel against perceived authority figures—including drug treatment counselors—without really thinking about their own needs or desires. An individually oriented treatment approach may make little sense to a person who attends to the needs of the family above his or her individual needs.

When a woman has no sense of hope, no sense of future, and a complete sense of personal disempowerment, the concept of "powerlessness" may not help her make the spiritual connection that is so important to successful recovery.

Many substance users will need help interpreting the culture of 12-step programs if the concepts are to make sense or be useful. Individual attention will be essential for such people as an adjunct to the group support of AA or other programs. Providers and community planners must be willing to try different approaches to recovery and treatment, to learn about models in other regions and adapt them to be appropriate for their own. Special efforts are needed to develop programs relevant to a variety of individuals and cultures.

A common quality of addicts and their family members is a sense of alienation and being different. "No one has ever had the problems I do. No one like me has ever succeeded in drug treatment or recovery."

People who do not identify with the dominant culture might easily believe this to be true if they look at a mainstream recovery program. They may see few women, people of color, gay men or lesbians, poor people, disabled people, youth or elders. This contributes to the sense of hopelessness and isolation these users already feel.

A program that welcomes a person or family will do this in part by being culturally "familiar" from the outset. People of color need to see and hear other people of color. Lesbians need to talk with other lesbians. Elders need support from other elders who can reassure them that the effort recovery demands is well worth it, even in one's senior years.

The visible presence of someone "like me" who is participating in a recovery program, or who is living a sober lifestyle, can be an immense aid in breaking through an individual's fear and denial of his or her chemical dependency.

Familiarity with cultural attitudes towards substance use and chemical dependency can also be useful in prevention, treatment and recovery efforts. For example, many leaders in the African American and Latino communities point out that open drug trading and its associated violence can be seen in poor communities in any major U.S. city, especially in housing projects and poor Black and Latino neighborhoods. Similar blatant dealing in middle class White neighborhoods would not be tolerated. The implication is that the lives of poor people of color are disposable, while those of Whites are not. If a provider understands this point of view, and plans the content of programs with this perspective in mind, it may be easier for members of those communities to join the prevention effort.

Some individuals, as mentioned earlier, have cut ties with their culture of origin and realigned themselves with the drug culture. It is important to help such people reconnect to their cultures of origin. Placing emphasis on the strength and beauty of that culture can enhance self-esteem and give people hope for the future.

Encouraging members of disenfranchised communities to acknowledge and discuss past experiences of racism, discrimination or oppression can help them begin to develop tools to deal with the consequences of those experiences in ways that do not involve the use of substances.

Realignment with a cultural identity can give added strength to an individual's motivation in treatment and ability to maintain sobriety. Without this sense of connection to other people, and a sense of shared experience of culture, family or recovery, it will be extremely difficult for someone to succeed in treatment.

When we work with children exposed to drugs and alcohol or with their drug-involved families, our ability to respect and validate their culture, and to adapt our messages of prevention and care to be consonant with that culture, will add strength to our efforts.

(See Appendix E for resources on discussing cultural differences with young children.)

Chapter 3

Crack Cocaine: The Worst Drug Ever?

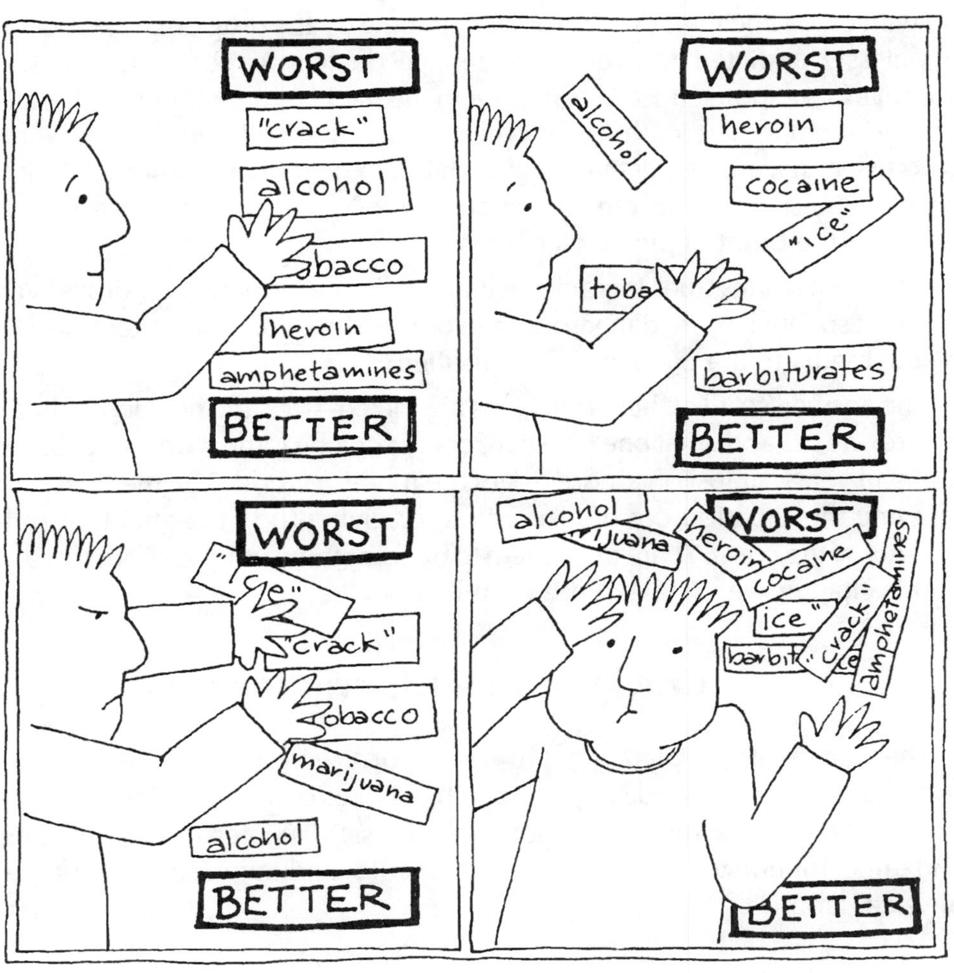

"I've read stories in the papers, seen features on the news about crack. It's like the people who are using it aren't even human, they can be so cruel. I hear it's the worst drug ever, the most addictive, and that it's everywhere. My own kids are only five and seven, but I worry about them incredibly. How will they be able to deal with this? What will happen to them if they try it some day?"

—Parent

Some of the worst horror stories any of us have heard in a long time have to do with crack cocaine. We are told that people try the drug once and become hopelessly addicted forever; that teenage dealers in possession of semi-automatic weapons shoot one another in the back, murder innocent bystanders and seem to care nothing for other people; that children born to women who use crack are aggressive, edgy, unable to be touched or loved; that the problem is especially severe in communities of color, and African Americans will bear the brunt of the crack epidemic.

Are these stories true? Is crack cocaine really worse than other drugs? What makes it so much more dangerous than other drugs, and is the attention given by the media to the crack problem justified?

The answers to all of these questions are mixed—yes and no. Depending on where one sits and what one has seen, crack cocaine is the worst drug to come along in years, or just one more risk of the modern world. The media is either blowing the situation out of proportion, or giving too little attention to the severity of the crisis. There does seem to be something unique about this drug. In this chapter we try to explore what it is.

Crack: A Brief Description

The leaves of the plant *Erythroxylum coca* were first chewed for their stimulant effect thousands of years ago by natives of the Peruvian highlands. The plant relieved symptoms of altitude sickness, alleviated feelings of hunger and thirst, minimized sensitivity to heat or cold, and increased endurance in physical labor.

Spaniards operating silver mines in Bolivia in the sixteenth century discovered that Indian slave laborers who chewed coca leaves worked longer hours with less food. German chemists, studying the plant in the nineteenth century, were successful in isolating its active ingredient, which they called "cocaine."

Cocaine experienced a surge of popularity in the late 1800s, and its beneficial effects were remarked on by many popular figures of the day. Satisfied users included Sigmund Freud, Queen Victoria, the Czar of Russia, President Ulysses S. Grant, Thomas Edison, Sarah Bernhardt, and even Pope Leo XIII.

Cocaine use was quite widespread in the United States and Europe by the beginning of the twentieth century, where it was a common ingredient in patent medicines and tonics sold door to door (including, of course, the original Coca-Cola). Around 1910, articles began to appear in newspapers and magazines expressing concern about the dangers of cocaine use. Cocaine related violence and deaths were reported. Tales were told of "respectable Christian men and women" becoming dope fiends who would engage in the most depraved behaviors imaginable to acquire more of the drug.

In an address to Congress, President William Howard Taft said, "Cocaine is more appalling in its effects than any other habit-forming drug used in the United States." The Harrison Act of 1914, the first federal anti-narcotics law, classified cocaine as a drug to be dispensed only by physicians under prescription. Soon, other legal measures were passed by federal and state governments to control the sale and use of cocaine and other substances.

It is ironic that we remember so poorly that earlier cocaine epidemic. In many ways, we are re-experiencing today some of the drug problems of a century ago. Cocaine use diminished for several decades, but became popular again throughout the 1970s. Cocaine addiction is not a new problem for this country.

Around the mid-1980s, the formula for an inexpensive form of smokable cocaine was popularized. A simple mixture of water, bicarbonate of soda and cocaine hydrochloride powder, formed into a paste, was dried in a microwave. The "rock" that resulted was smoked in a pipe. As it burned, the rock cocaine made a cracking noise. The drug was christened with the street name "crack."

When cocaine is smoked, the lungs quickly absorb the drug into the bloodstream. Because the lungs can absorb cocaine more quickly than the nasal passages, the blood levels of cocaine among crack smokers are considerably higher than among people who "snort" cocaine.

The crack high is immediate and more intense, but it is also short-lived (ten to forty minutes). The "fall" after using can be sudden and devastating. To avoid the painful depression that follows the high, crack users often binge. This repetitive behavior, along with the intrinsic properties of the drug, easily leads to dependence and addiction.

Crack cocaine is cheap to produce and relatively inexpensive to buy. When crack first appeared on the streets, a rock could be purchased for five or ten dollars. A binge session might cost as little as fifty dollars—considerably less than the thousands of dollars required for freebasing or injecting cocaine.

The greatest significance of the development of crack was the placement of what is probably the most addictive form of cocaine into the hands of a full range of consumers, from all classes and all backgrounds. Cocaine use, and the subsequent problems of cocaine addiction, were no longer the sole province of the middle and upper class.

How Addictive Is Crack Cocaine?

Cocaine produces extremely pleasant sensations. It was known as an especially addictive drug even before a smokable form was widely available. One researcher at the Addiction Research Center in Baltimore described cocaine as "the most powerful reinforcer known."*

In addiction studies, test animals learn to self-administer cocaine more quickly than any other drug, and, given the opportunity, they will continue to do so until they overdose and die. There is little question that crack is a terribly dangerous drug, and the risk of a casual user developing a dependency is great.

However, there are individuals who have been casual users— smoking a little crack once or twice a week—for a number of years. They function reasonably well in family and society, and they use the drug with restraint.

There are also individuals who have used crack heavily for several weeks

* Michael Kuhar, cited by Holden (1989), p. 1378.

or months, and then managed to stop using it entirely on their own, without the help of a treatment program. And there are crack users who have recognized their dependency, entered treatment and been successful in stopping use altogether.

> "This crack thing has been really complicated. I do drug prevention work with youth, so when the stories about crack first came out, there I was warning them all: 'Don't try this drug. Don't even try it once! One time is all it takes to get addicted, and if you try it, you'll probably get hooked immediately. Once you're hooked, it's almost impossible to get off it.'
>
> "I'm not the only source of information for these kids, of course. They check out the scene with people who've tried the drug too. And they find out that it isn't one hundred percent addictive, that there are a fair number of casual users out there, that some people have gotten pretty hooked on crack for a while and then stopped using it when things got too weird for them.
>
> "I know that crack is an extraordinarily addictive drug, and that it's really dangerous for the youth I work with to try it. But I lost a lot of credibility because I hadn't been telling them the truth. They're starting to trust me again now, but it's taken some time."
>
> —Youth outreach worker

The fact that some people have been able to use crack "moderately," and that others have been successful at ending use when they felt it was necessary to do so, does not diminish the overall danger of the drug.

Patterns of addiction are established quickly with crack. An individual with even a mild predilection to dependency is likely to develop uncontrollable cravings for crack in a matter of days. The great majority of crack addicts who have sought treatment have found it an extraordinarily difficult dependency to break.

The best choice for any individual is never to try the drug. Still, it is important to be balanced in our representation of its effects—the risk of addiction is considerable for those who use the drug. It is, however, a risk and not a certainty.

Is Crack Causing More Crime?

> "We are seeing alarming increases in violence and criminal behavior in our community related to crack cocaine. There are few neighborhoods in the city that are not being affected in some way—we've seen the incidence of murder, burglary and robbery rise. I worry that if the trend continues, in a few years there will not be a safe time of day or night anywhere in town."
>
> —Police officer

Drug-related violence is not new. Liquor wars during prohibition were notorious for their disregard for human life, and innocent bystanders were frequent victims of shootings and bombings by rival gangs. Execution-style killings by organized crime figures have been carried out against individuals who moved into an already-claimed market to sell heroin, marijuana or LSD.

Using and dealing any number of substances have long carried the stigma of illegality. For decades, addicts have committed crimes to obtain enough money to buy drugs. Has crack really brought us anything different?

Along with the rise in popularity of crack cocaine has been a disturbing rise in inner-city violence and heightened activity in the international cocaine trade. Drug markets once monopolized by local organized crime and international drug cartels have now been opened to teen gangs and small-time dealers. The competition is tough and vicious. The players in this terrible drama are armed and dangerous.

Teenagers who have not fully developed a sense of personal morality, of good and bad or of right and wrong are easily influenced by the moral impoverishment of the drug culture. The culture's violence and disregard for human life quickly become accepted norms.

Like other times in history that young people have been given considerable power in immoral societies (Hitler's Nazi youth, the Khmer Rouge in Cambodia), some of these teenagers have proven themselves capable of committing atrocities. Those who are also using the product they sell are likely to become irritable, impulsive, paranoid and even psychotic with chronic use.

These circumstances have created a situation prone to repeated outbursts of devastating violence. What is new about the violence related to the crack trade is that it is widespread; it involves many young people and petty dealers; chronic cocaine use can increase an individual's propensity to violence; and the trade lacks the regulation, negotiation and controls imposed by the more traditional organized crime families.

When Pregnant Women Use Crack

> "These little tiny babies, rigid and stiff, crying all the time, having seizures. It is really heartbreaking. I think crack cocaine has been responsible for some of the most messed up babies I've ever seen."
>
> —Pediatric nurse

When pregnant women use crack cocaine, their fetuses are placed in considerable danger. This is a very disturbing consequence of the crack epidemic. Infants who have experienced prenatal cocaine exposure may be anxious and irritable. Some have difficulty feeding and gaining weight.

Prenatal or neonatal seizures may occur, causing significant and sometimes permanent brain damage. As the children grow, they may be awkward and uncoordinated, and they may develop mild to severe learning disabilities.

One of the physiologic effects of cocaine use is constriction of circulation. A pregnant woman who smokes crack will experience constriction of blood flow to the placenta. When the drug crosses the placental barrier, the fetus may suffer constricted blood flow to its brain.

Cocaine is unique in its profound effect on the placenta and its ability to cause fetal hypoxia (oxygen deprivation). This is the likely explanation for the neurologic difficulties infants exposed to crack sometimes show.

At present, we cannot say how many children born to mothers who use crack will be affected, and of those who are, how many will be severely affected, and how many will be moderately or mildly affected. We do not have enough information to confidently predict the developmental potential of a child affected by crack.

We cannot successfully separate out the specific effects of crack cocaine from the effects of other substances used during pregnancy. Yet, with all we do not know or cannot do, we *can* say with absolute certainty that crack cocaine is an extremely dangerous drug for a pregnant woman to use.

When Pregnant Women Use Alcohol, Tobacco and Other Drugs

It is curious that crack has received the considerable attention it has in light of the limited attention given to other substances used with even greater frequency by pregnant women—substances which also cause problems for the fetus or newborn.

Fetal alcohol syndrome (FAS), for example, is caused by prenatal exposure to alcohol. It is the leading cause of mental retardation in the United States; an estimated 40,000 children a year are born with some type of alcohol-related birth defect. As with other kinds of prenatal chemical exposure, some of these children are mildly and others severely affected. Those with severe FAS are significantly disabled. In the newborn period, they are likely to have difficulties with feeding and growth.

Some children with FAS will be diagnosed with cardiac or other organ abnormalities and be slowed in developmental milestones. Older children may have difficulty understanding and processing new information or cause-and-effect relationships, be impulsive in some of their behaviors, and have fine and/or gross motor incoordination. As children with FAS mature, they may have increasingly limited social capabilities and be unable to live independently as adults.

Smoking also presents significant risks to fetuses. Pregnant women who smoke are at increased risk for miscarriage, difficulties during labor and prematurity. Their children are more likely to be born prematurely and be small for their gestational age.

Children who were prenatally exposed to tobacco are at greater risk of sudden infant death syndrome (SIDS), are more likely to grow slowly and have learning disabilities and behavioral problems, and have a higher frequency of respiratory diseases in their first five years (usually related to exposure to secondary smoke).

The extraordinary attention placed on crack cocaine has distracted attention that could be usefully focused on other dangerous substances as well, especially alcohol and tobacco. It has focused our energies on a specific drug instead of maintaining a broad-based concern for substance abuse generally. It has placed an emphasis on "them," outsiders who use illicit drugs, and allowed us to avoid looking at "us" and the greater acceptance of drinking and smoking.

There is no question that crack use during pregnancy is very dangerous for mother and fetus. For the well-being of both, it should not be used. But pregnant women should also be discouraged from using other substances that might harm a developing fetus, including alcohol, cigarettes, illicit recreational drugs and certain kinds of over-the-counter or prescription drugs.

The Crack Epidemic and Communities of Color

"I"ve been asked to speak to teachers about the crisis of crack-exposed children entering the schools. I've been invited to special classrooms working with behaviorally disordered children. I'm told that many of the younger children are suspected of being crack-exposed kids.

"You know what I see when I get there? Classrooms full of black and brown children.

"White folks are using crack cocaine, too. Their children have had prenatal exposure, too. Their families are chaotic and dysfunctional, too. So where are their crack-exposed children? They're out there in the regular school classes. They're not considered 'behaviorally disordered.'

"I fear these 'problems' are being diagnosed because the schools simply do not know how to work with children of color."

—Public health administrator

The inner cities *are* being devastated by crack cocaine, and this includes poor African American and Latino neighborhoods. The development of this cheap form of high, made widely available with such ease, coincided with some disquieting economic trends.

In the 1980s, the distinctions between the classes increased— the poor got poorer and the rich got richer. More families in the lower middle class slipped into poverty. Rates of unemployment rose. Drug prevention and treatment programs were cut. Opportunities, especially for poor people with limited educational attainment, decreased.

Many people without jobs and without hope had free time on their hands. This created an atmosphere especially conducive to the development of chemical dependencies. This population was vulnerable when crack cocaine arrived on the scene, and the effects of the crack trade are clearly visible in many inner-city neighborhoods.

However, it would be a mistake to assume that middle class, suburban or rural communities are not also affected by crack cocaine. People in these communities are using as well. The major distinction is the lower visibility of crack in middle class communities.

While *use* may be fairly common across socioeconomic and racial lines, the actual trade of crack is predominantly confined to the inner city and to poor neighborhoods. It is fairly easy for a determined observer—a news reporter, for example—to find significant evidence of crack use among African Americans or Latinos in those neighborhoods. The privilege of the middle class allows their usage to remain more discrete.

Substance Abuse: The Greater Problem

There are many dramatic and horrible stories about crack cocaine. There is much that is frightening, much that is alarming and much that demands thoughtful and comprehensive response. But what crack cocaine brings us is not all new, and the problems are not unsolvable. Why, then, has this drug received so much attention and concern?

In the public's mind (and the media's presentations), crack is identified as a problem of disenfranchised populations, particularly poor African Americans and Latinos. Crack is strongly associated with illegal activity and crime.

And, though this perception is not correct, it is not considered a direct problem of middle class neighborhoods, nor is it generally considered a problem among Anglo populations. Crack cocaine is "their" problem, an outside issue that does not affect neighbors and friends.

Alcohol, on the other hand, is a widely used legal substance. Neighbors, friends and family may all use it. An individual watching the latest news report on the dangers of crack cocaine may well be doing so over an after-work beer. During the commercial break, he or she may flip the pages of a weekly news magazine, skimming over advertisements for scotch and vodka. Alcohol is not so foreign to the middle class. It is also responsible for greater numbers of health problems in adults and newborns, more highway injuries and deaths, and greater financial costs to society than crack cocaine.

While the wide attention given to crack has been helpful in some respects, it has also hindered our ability to keep a balanced perspective on the greater problem of substance abuse generally. This is a problem that touches nearly every individual in the country in some way.

We must establish programs to treat and prevent all forms of substance abuse and all forms of prenatal chemical exposure. We must do everything we can to help our children grow up drug free. We cannot solve the problem of crack addiction without also addressing the problems of alcoholism, marijuana use, cigarette smoking or heroin dependence. If one substance becomes unavailable, the chemically dependent person will simply find another to use in its place.

We believe that intensive prevention and treatment campaigns *will* have a positive effect on the problem of prenatal chemical exposure. It is important for society in general, and providers working with children especially, to look clearly and honestly at the broad scope of these problems and respond in thoughtful and aggressive ways. Chemical dependency is a problem that affects all of us, whatever neighborhood we might live in.

❧ ❧ ❧

Michael
A Toddler with a Loving Foster Mother

Michael came in for his first clinic visit at age 13 months, accompanied by his new foster mother, Anna-Marie. His birth mother had used crack cocaine during her pregnancy, but there was no other information available on her pregnancy or his birth. He had been placed in foster care immediately upon release from the hospital, in a home with three other children exposed prenatally to cocaine. His original foster mother complained that Michael was aggressive, hostile and uncontrollable. She was unable to continue caring for him and returned him to the department of social services.

Michael had been living with Anna-Marie for one week and was the only child in the home. He was extremely small for his age—in fact, he was one of the smallest children his age ever seen in the clinic (well below the third percentile for height and weight). His head size was normal and he was physically quite agile, but his speech was markedly delayed. He did not talk or even babble. He communicated primarily through screaming.

Anna-Marie was hoping to get suggestions for Michael's care. Like his first foster mother, she had had difficulty feeding the boy, getting him to sleep, holding him and calming him. She was an experienced foster mother who had cared for a number of children, but none had been as demanding or difficult as Michael. She had not seen him sleep a single time while he had been in her care. If she put him in his crib, he rolled from side to side and screamed the entire time he was there. On a number of occasions, he had actually thrown himself out of the crib and had fallen to the floor. Anna-Marie herself was exhausted from lack of sleep.

Michael was unusually active during his clinic visit. He was difficult to examine. He would not sit still in Anna-Marie's lap. He cried constantly. His cry was unusual—screechy in quality and painful to hear. He turned his face away from the doctor, avoided eye contact, and pulled away from the stethoscope and otoscope. On three occasions in this short visit, he threw himself onto the ground, screaming and banging his head on the floor.

Anna-Marie was given recommendations for Michael's care. She was encouraged to set a highly regimented schedule for Michael, explaining each part of the day to him as they went along: "Now it is nap time. Now it is time to eat. Now it is time to play." Transitions to new activities were to be made carefully and deliberately, giving Michael a short "warning" before moving to a new activity.

To help with Michael's feeding, small, frequent, high-calorie meals were recommended. Anna-Marie was given a list of easy-to-chew and easy-to-prepare foods for Michael that included bananas, whole-milk yogurt, rice and tapioca.

Michael's crib needed some modifications to make it a safe place for him to rest. He needed bumper cushions all around the crib, as well as a safety net over the top. After feeding, he was to be given five minute rest time. Throughout the day, he was to be set down for other short naps. Because Michael seemed especially fearful of being left alone, Anna-Marie was encouraged to lie down in the room with him during these short naps. At night, his bedroom was to have a couple of soft night lights—the goal was to have the room lit comfortably so that it was neither overbright nor especially dark.

Because Michael was a medically fragile child (a child with a significantly disabling medical condition), Anna-Marie was eligible for a special respite-care program in the county. The clinic staff made the necessary arrangements for her to have a couple of periods during the week when she could take a break from Michael.

Follow-up: Because of Michael's slow growth, he was seen weekly for the next month. At the first follow-up visit, Anna-Marie was already finding it easier to feed him, his weight gain was quite good, and he had begun sleeping more easily and regularly. By the fourth follow-up visit, Michael's attachment to Anna-Marie was evident and growing. He had become more interested in food, but continued to be excited during feeding. On a number of occasions, he had thrown entire plates of food across the room. His excellent aim attested to his improving fine motor skills. Visits were set up on a monthly basis after this.

At these monthly visits various aspects of Michael's development and health status were evaluated. He continued to grow physically stronger and to strengthen his fine and gross motor skills. Though his speech and language skills remained delayed, he was increasingly able to use language to communicate. Over time, he also became somewhat better at monitoring his own behavior and his aggressiveness and impulsivity decreased. Because Anna-Marie had seen such improvement in Michael's behavior and skill levels, she was generally pleased with his development. However, Michael's behavior was not always as easy for others to manage.

When Michael was 18 months old, Anna-Marie enrolled him in a community daycare program to give him social experience with other children. At first, Michael had a great deal of difficulty relating appropriately to the other children in his class. He was aggressive and bit other children on two occasions. His teachers were as frustrated with him as Anna-Marie had been at first.

Anna-Marie spoke to his teachers and suggested ways of working successfully with Michael. She arranged to spend time in the classroom to demonstrate the effective behavior management techniques and positive reinforcement strategies that she had employed with him. She helped the staff understand how to set limits with Michael, prepare him for transitions, hold him properly, and so on. She continued to spend time in the classroom on a regular basis, providing individual attention for Michael during the difficult periods of the day. Anna-Marie's ability to communicate Michael's needs and her willingness to work with his teachers helped to create a positve environment for him, and his preschool experience was ultimately a successful one.

Comment: *Michael showed many of the more severe symptoms of prenatal cocaine exposure. Proper care of Michael was time-consuming and demanding. His social skills were especially discouraging. He was not an easy child to like as a toddler, and he did not get along with other children. However, by the time he was three, providers who had watched Michael from an early age were amazed at the extent of his progress. No one who had evaluated him when he first came into the clinic would have predicted such marked improvements in language and social behaviors.*

The importance of consistent and loving care is seen in Michael's story. Long-term placement with a loving, skillful foster parent has been of immeasurable benefit to Michael, and Anna-Marie and the clinic staff can all be reasonably hopeful about this boy's future.

❧ ❧ ❧

Chapter 4

Chemical Dependency: A Disease, Not a Crime

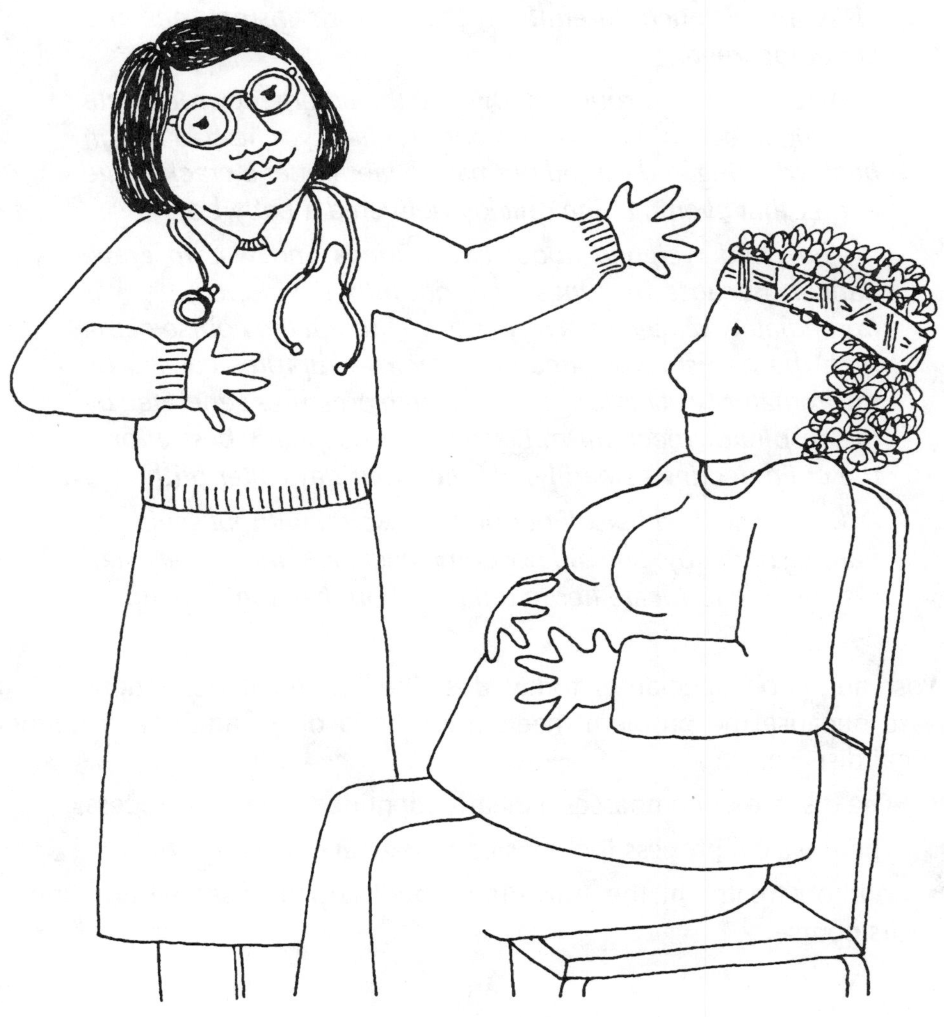

Kathy, 18 years old, had participated in several earnest discussions with the clinic obstetrician. She was pregnant with her third child. Her two other children were in foster care.

Kathy had used alcohol and drugs during her prior pregnancies, and one of her children, the three year old, was markedly delayed in development.

Kathy promised the doctor she was staying clean for this pregnancy, saying she was older now, more mature and ready to be a good mother. She showed up for most of her prenatal visits and listened carefully to the doctor's instructions and encouragement.

An ambulance brought Kathy into the emergency room late one night, seven months into her pregnancy. She had begun hemorrhaging and started premature labor after a crack binge earlier that evening. She quickly delivered a baby boy.

The child weighed about two pounds and was in grave danger. Because his lungs were not fully developed, he was immediately placed on a respirator. Through the course of the night he had several pneumothoracies—ruptures caused by the immaturity of his lungs and the high pressures generated by the respirator mechanism.Despite the hospital's best efforts, the child declined steadily. He died four days after birth.

Kathy checked herself out of the hospital without seeing or naming her baby. She did not come back, and the nursery staff was unable to locate her to tell her about her son's death.

Most addiction specialists today describe chemical dependency as a disease because the problem meets the criteria of a traditionally defined medical disease:

- The disease encompasses a clearly identified physical process.
- The physical process includes pathological effects.
- Without treatment, the individual cannot stop the disease from running its course.

Chemical dependency has many physiologic effects, and chronic substance use may lead to a progressive deterioration of several different organ systems. Which organ systems are affected, and the manner in which they are affected, varies depending on the substance used. The disease process of chemical dependency can be *arrested* by abstinence, but the chemically dependent person is never *cured* of the disease.

For the chemically dependent person, the compulsion to drink or use drugs is overwhelming. It is not affected by moral beliefs, character, personal willpower or intention. The individual cannot control the compulsion to use.

Chemical dependency is considered a medical problem by the American Medical Association, the American Psychiatric Association, the American Hospital Association, the United States Congress and the United States Surgeon General. Medical associations advise against punitive approaches in responding to substance abuse.

> "I'm a health care provider, and my function is to treat illness and disease. The best possible response I can offer people who are dependent on alcohol or drugs is to treat their illness. I'm here to help and to support. I don't condone their use of substance, and I encourage them to enter recovery or treatment. But I also sympathize with my chemically dependent patients. Many of them want very much to be free of the compulsion to use. Their drug no longer offers them euphoria. It's just an essential part of their survival. When you meet addicts and alcoholics in this state, you can really see the disease process clearly. These are very sick people, and they are suffering terribly."
>
> —Physician

Using the disease model when addiction is at issue offers the greatest hope for the chemically dependent person. With the assistance of support groups, church- and community-based programs, treatment and recovery agencies, and 12-step programs, such as Alcoholics Anonymous (AA) or Narcotics Anonymous (NA), many chemically dependent people have been able to find help and develop a drug-abstinent lifestyle.

The Need for Care and Treatment

Health care workers share a common goal in wanting to help pregnant women maintain health practices that are good for mother and fetus. It is essential that pregnant women see their providers as allies in this effort. This builds the bond of trust that allows a pregnant woman to admit to difficulties she faces in her health practices.

A pregnant woman may be coping with any number of health-related issues: nutritional deficits, cigarette smoking, drinking, crack use, poverty, undereducation, unemployment. When informed of these problems, providers can endeavor to offer assistance. They can use their knowledge, skills and resources to help build trust with the patient, provide her the services she needs, refer her to other systems of support, validate her health-seeking behaviors, and set the foundation for positive mother-infant bonding that will be critical to the child's well-being.

Unfortunately, the ideal range of services is not available to many women in need. The pregnant woman who seeks treatment for chemical dependency faces particular challenges. There is a shortage of placements in drug and alcohol programs across the board, and many prospective clients must wait months for an opening.

There is an additional shortage of placements in programs that serve women, so women usually have to wait even longer than men to enter treatment—periods during which a pregnant addict or alcoholic continues to use substances and the developing fetus continues to be exposed to danger.

Few residential programs include housing for children, so women with children often must give them up to foster care for the duration of their treatment or recovery program. This means involving Child Protective Services and risking permanent custody loss.

Furthermore, foster placements may separate siblings, and children may be placed a considerable distance away from each other and their family. A woman without a car may be physically unable to visit children one or two counties away.

Mothers who were placed in foster care during their own childhood may have painful memories of the uncertainty and confusion they experienced. In some cases, they were physically or sexually abused during foster care. There are cases where foster children have been treated differently from biological children; they may be fed different meals made of less expensive foods, dressed in cast-offs, given beds in the least favorable part of the house, and so forth.

Considering all of these factors, many chemically-dependent women with young children feel the best choice for the welfare of their family and children is to stay out of treatment and away from the view of Child Protective Services.

There are almost no treatment programs that serve chemically dependent pregnant women. The complications of withdrawal during pregnancy, the dangers to the fetus, and the risks of lawsuits have made programs wary of such clients. Pregnant teenagers face the greatest difficulty finding placement. In some cases, women accepted to treatment programs who were later discovered to be pregnant have been asked to leave.

It is tragic but true that most pregnant women with chemical dependencies are not admitted to treatment or recovery programs even if they discuss the matter with their physicians or care providers, are highly motivated, and have private insurance that would cover the costs of such treatment. For pregnant women, the necessary programs just don't exist.*

Criminalizing Chemical Dependency

In recent years, attempts to invoke laws to punish pregnant women for "fetal abuse" have surfaced around the country. These have included such charges as involuntary manslaughter (against a woman whose newborn child died, allegedly because of complications arising from her use of cocaine during pregnancy); second-degree child abuse and delivering cocaine to a child (against a woman whose newborn tested positive for cocaine at the time of birth); and "willful failure to provide medical attention to a minor child" (against a woman who continued to use amphetamines during her pregnancy despite her doctor's advice to stop).

Some of these cases have been successfully prosecuted. Those who participate in the prosecutions insist they have the welfare of children at heart,

* Recently, a federal agency, the Office of Substance Abuse Prevention (OSAP), has recognized the need for specialized treatment programs serving pregnant women with chemical dependency. Programs have been funded in several states. We hope this trend will continue and grow.

and that these drastic measures are necessary to protect fetuses or newborns who cannot protect themselves.

Certainly the issue is not an easy one. But we believe the efforts at criminalization, well-meaning though they may be, ultimately harm more than they help. They are based on a number of common misunderstandings about what will happen if pregnant substance abusers are prosecuted and incarcerated.

Pregnant Women in the Prison System

Many believe the threat of prosecution will convince pregnant women to stop using drugs. No deterrent effect has been demonstrated from enforcing "fetal abuse" statutes. More to the point, providers commonly report that women fearful of prosecution are likely to misrepresent or deny any drug use in their history, fail to seek treatment for dependencies or avoid prenatal care altogether.

There is a common belief that pregnant women in jail or prison will receive adequate prenatal care—better care, in fact, than they would receive outside the system. While some correctional facilities may have a properly staffed and funded medical unit, most do not.

Care for incarcerated pregnant women is likely to be irregular and inconsistent, often provided by personnel poorly trained in obstetrical medicine. Nutrition in prisons is generally poor. Parenting education is limited, and mental health support is often non-existent except in the most extreme crises of suicidal behavior or violence. A prison or jail is far from an ideal setting for maintaining and promoting the health of a pregnant woman.

Another common belief is that pregnant substance abusers will not have access to drugs in the correctional system and will receive drug treatment services. Again, the facts are much more somber. Drugs and alcohol are widely available and widely used in many prisons and jails. Women without money to buy drugs may trade sex for substances. Drug treatment programs are scarce. The community and culture within the correctional system are not "clean and sober," and support for sobriety and recovery is usually non-existent.

Some who advocate the incarceration of pregnant women with chemical dependencies acknowledge this is not a perfect solution, but feel there are no viable alternatives.

Treatment and recovery services for pregnant women are scarce. But the financial investment represented by incarceration is considerably greater than the cost to place the same woman in a community-based drug treatment or alcohol recovery program. Better options could be made available, most notably by recognizing chemical dependency as a medical problem rather than a legal one, and responding with medical care rather than legal punishment.

The Case Against Prosecution

> "You have to understand that most women using drugs and alcohol are already distrustful of 'the system.' We have a government official at the highest level of the so-called drug war who has suggested we take the children of drug-using parents away from their families and place them in orphanages. What a terrifying threat! These women are very attached to their kids, and being a mother is really important to them.
>
> "I spend a lot of time with patients at my clinic convincing them I am an ally, that they can trust me, that we are working together to do what's best for them and their babies. If word got out that I was reporting women who were using, and they were getting in trouble with the law and ending up in jail, they just wouldn't come to see me. If there were an emergency and they had to come, they wouldn't ever tell me they were using drugs. I would be missing some incredibly important information I need to provide good health care for mother and fetus."
>
> —Obstetrical nurse

Because of the paucity of proper treatment and recovery programs, a chemically dependent pregnant woman often faces only two choices: she can continue to use, or she can stop using and go through withdrawal without care or treatment. Both options are dangerous for the fetus. Unmonitored withdrawal may be life-threatening for both mother and fetus. Additionally, most chemically dependent women have tried to stop using on their own many times, without success. It should not surprise us that without treatment options, most pregnant addicts and alcoholics continue to use.

Women dealing with chemical dependencies are extremely sensitive to judgment from providers, and are especially wary of the criminal justice system. If they feel they are in any danger of prosecution by admitting their drug or alcohol use in a prenatal program, they may attempt to conceal their substance use from providers. Women with private insurance may go to suburban hospitals in middle class areas that do not screen as carefully for substance use.

Many women will avoid all prenatal care. Their guilt and remorse over the "criminality" of their behavior may actually lead to increased use and greater danger for the fetus—one survey of pregnant crack users showed they were aware of the dangers to the fetus and used more crack to avoid the discomfort raised by such knowledge.

Women who fear prosecution for drug use during pregnancy will often choose to deliver in out-of-hospital settings. Their infants will be three times more likely to die in the first year of life than those born with prenatal care and appropriate delivery services.

The population most likely to be affected by so-called fetal abuse statutes are women who are already outside of the health care system. They are young and low-income, and those most commonly prosecuted so far have been women of color.

Medical Intervention: A Strategy That Works

"Your story about Kathy, the crack-using mother who abandoned her dying newborn, is typical of others we've heard. Actually, I could tell you many stories worse than that one.

"Well, we can tell all the horror stories we want. While they may be actual accounts, they do not necessarily tell the truth. The truth is that most of these families care deeply about their children. Usually, the whole family rallies around a seriously ill infant. Grandmothers, aunts, father and mother are devastated by the circumstances, and if the child dies they feel a deep ache of loss.

"If the infant survives the critical phase, other questions loom for the family: Will the child have further crises, physical problems, developmental delay? Will the family be able to cope with chronic illness or developmental problems?

"Facing these uncertainties, the families are extremely grateful for the patience, knowledge and hope the health care team can offer. They need to know the team will continue to be there to help the family learn about this child and give him or her the best chance possible. Knowing the team will be there for the next few months, the next few years—maybe even throughout the child's life—can make it easier for all of them to take the risk of devoting themselves to this child's very best potentials."

—Physician

Medical intervention is an effective strategy that can help pregnant addicts and alcoholics cope with their dependencies, support the health of the developing fetus, and strengthen the family bonds, providing a great resource to the child. Such intervention does not solve all problems and cannot relieve all suffering. But well-designed and properly funded programs of treatment, recovery and care can have an immensely positive effect on a community's problem of substance abuse, and might have a considerable influence on the problem of prenatal chemical exposure.

Criminalization puts health care providers in a position where they must police and punish patients who come to them for help in the care and treatment of a medical disease. Such actions are antithetical to the most fundamental premises of proper medical care. Criminalization drives women away from treatment and further jeopardizes the well-being of an already at-risk fetus. It may influence some women to increase the frequency and dosage of substance use.

Ultimately, criminalization of pregnant women's chemical dependencies will fail as a strategy in the "drug war" because it compounds rather than corrects the problem. Furthermore, it diverts us from the more pragmatic tasks of understanding and treating chemical dependency and creating a society where we emphasize prevention rather than prosecution of this medical disease.

Chapter 5

Helping the Family, Helping the Child

"When I first started providing psychotherapy to children, I was really excited. The children were fun and creative and easy to spend time with. I liked them a lot, and I loved doing play therapy!

"I never really wanted to work with adults, and I had a very hard time with the parents of some of my child clients. I knew they could be cruel to their kids and very selfish about their own needs. I would see parents occasionally because it was required, but I wasn't especially sympathetic or supportive.

"It took me a while to realize I wasn't helping any of the children I was seeing if I couldn't also be a friend and ally to their parents. In a lot of cases, the children didn't even need to be in therapy and the parents did. My wonderful, fun child therapy cases would turn into difficult and dreary adult cases.

"With time and experience, I've learned to care about and respect the parents more, and to have a better sense of the struggles they face. I still think of myself as working with children. But I accomplish this mainly by doing the best work I can with mothers and fathers who need help understanding their children's capabilities and learning to parent their children more consistently."

—Marriage, family and child counselor

We can expect that many children with prenatal drug or alcohol exposure will grow up in families affected by the disease of chemical dependency. When one member of a family exhibits a chemical dependency, all other family members are affected in some way even if they do not use substances themselves. It is useful to understand the family effects of chemical dependency when working with children from drug- or alcohol-involved families.

Often, this will help providers intervene with family members in ways that will be more effective than focusing on the individual child. At other times, knowing how chemical dependency affects family members may help improve understanding of a particular child's experiences, behavior or feelings.

Who Are the Families?

Each family, like each child, is unique. It has a unique set of circumstances, strengths and challenges. We can describe trends and generalities, but it is essential to remember that every family, like every child, will need careful individual assessment.

We commonly hear that chemical dependency presents a particular challenge among poor families, especially in communities of color. Chemical dependency does not respond to lines of class or ethnicity. Research suggests that equal numbers of children are born drug exposed in public and private hospitals, and among Whites as well as African Americans.

What *does* distinguish middle class and wealthy families from working class and poor is the matter of resources. Families with more money often have resources that are not available to those with less. They may have private insurance that can pay the costs of recovery or treatment programs—their wait for treatment will be shorter than the family without insurance.

The state tends to be less intrusive and punitive with middle class families. Doctors are less likely to report them for child abuse or neglect, and the criminal justice system is less likely to charge them with crimes related to substance use.

With the financial resources available to them, middle class and wealthy users are less likely to resort to criminal behavior to pay for their dependencies. They are more likely to have a system of regular childcare in place, so they are freed up to use drugs or spend time purchasing illegal drugs without physically abandoning their children. Overall, they are simply better able to camouflage the effects and indications of chemical dependency.

Typical Problems in the Affected Family

A number of typical problems arise in families affected by chemical dependency. Children are sensitive to these difficulties and may exhibit behaviors related to the distress they feel about their family's problems. The following are some of the most common problems.

Financial. Drug and alcohol use costs money. The substance user must divert financial resources that could contribute to the family. Use of the substance may make it difficult to perform at work. As the disease progresses, sick leave is used up, work performance declines and jobs may be lost. It may become impossible for the user to work at all. Bills pile up, needed items are not purchased, the family may be unable to pay for proper food or medical care. Even middle class and wealthy families often run into financial difficulties as the disease of chemical dependency progresses.

Social. Social outlets for the user and the family often become increasingly constricted. More and more emphasis is placed on spending time with people who can help acquire drugs or who will share in their use. The user becomes less interested in social activities not related to use, and is less likely to attend events such as children's sporting events, school plays, neighborhood picnics, church socials, etc. Embarrassment or uncertainty about how the user may behave often leads family members to stop inviting people to the home. Children with a chemically dependent parent often do not invite friends over after school, for example. The user may also be embarrassed or ashamed of his/her dependency, and find it difficult to spend time around non-users.

Violence. As the disease progresses, some addicts/alcoholics develop diminished impulse control and become increasingly violent. Spouse and child abuse may occur during episodes of use. Easy access to guns or other weapons may contribute to impulsive violence ending in killings or serious injuries.

As an individual gets more involved in use of an illegal substance, he or she is more likely to become involved in selling and dealing. These activities always bring the user and his or her family one step closer to the violence of turf wars, retribution and power plays. "Friends" who are users or dealers may also be involved in violent and criminal activities. The family's overall exposure to violence increases.

In poor, inner-city neighborhoods which have become a center for drug dealing, violence is epidemic. Middle class users move through the neighborhood to buy drugs, and then return to their own safer neighborhoods. Poor people, whether they are users or not, have to keep living in the areas where drug dealing takes place. In some areas, children sleep on floors or in bathtubs because nightly shootings have left bullet holes in the walls of their homes. Children (and adults) may witness incredible acts of violence which disturb them deeply and disrupt their lives.

Physical health. Physical problems always accompany chronic use of alcohol or drugs. Different substances affect the body in different ways, and significant organ system damage may result from chronic use. Alcoholics may suffer liver damage. Injection drug users may develop blood infections or suffer heart valve destruction. Cigarette smokers have an increased risk of lung cancer. Users of phencycladine (PCP), LSD, cocaine or alcohol may lose cognitive ability and function. Injuries are suffered due to automobile accidents or falls during use.

Chemically dependent individuals are likely to ignore signs of illness, and typically show up in acute crisis in emergency rooms for conditions which might have been easily and successfully treated if responded to earlier.

Users may also suffer physical problems as a result of overuse in a single episode (overdose), combining substances, or use of substances cut with dangerous extenders. Barbiturate users, for example, may experience depression of heart rate, blood pressure or respiration, leading in some cases to death. Users of opiates often experience nausea or vomiting immediately after ingesting drugs, and with an overdose may suffer respiratory arrest and death. In combination with alcohol, the danger of respiratory arrest from opiate or barbiturate use is especially acute.

The health of other family members is also affected by chemical dependency. Like the user, they are likely to ignore symptoms of ill health. Considerable energy and focus is given to the family's need to maintain denial or attend to the demands of the user. To divert attention from these efforts by seeking medical attention may feel disloyal or improper. Additionally, doctors' visits are costly, and the family may be struggling financially.

Members of a family affected by chemical dependency can suffer a variety of stress-related symptoms. Nutritional problems may arise because the family is unable to afford appropriate food or is too disorganized to purchase food and prepare meals. Where there is family violence, injuries related to physical abuse may occur.

HIV infection (infection with the AIDS virus) is sometimes present in a family member who has used injection drugs or crack cocaine. Injection drug users can be infected through needle sharing, and crack users have been infected through sexual intercourse with others who carry the virus. Infants may be born with HIV if their mother had the virus during her pregnancy.

HIV is not casually transmitted, but it may be found among several members of a family when one or both parents use injection drugs or smoke crack. Because chemical dependency is often widespread within a single family, there have in fact been instances where HIV develops in a father, mother, aunt or uncle, adult cousin, and one or more children. Chronic illness, especially one as severe as HIV, complicates already-difficult family situations.

Children born after prenatal drug exposure may have long-term, chronic health problems, occasionally of considerable severity. There may be lengthy hospitalizations in the neonatal period, frequent follow-up medical visits and a need for specialized home care. A child's physical and cognitive development may be slowed, requiring careful attendance in feeding, diapering and play for years longer than usual. These circumstances place further demands on families already stretched to their limits.

Mental health. During episodes of use, substances typically affect the user's emotion and mood, and often influence short-term memory, depth perception, attention and concentration. There are also specific mental disorders which may arise as a result of substance use. For example, cocaine users may experience episodes of psychosis after a few months of heavy use.

A single episode of LSD use can result in acute psychotic episodes in which users are a danger to themselves or others. Withdrawal from alcohol or amphetamines may also lead to psychotic episodes. Marijuana users sometimes report paranoid feelings or anxiety. Chronic use of virtually any substance will lead to a decreased ability in problem solving and some loss of cognitive capacity.

As the situation worsens, members of the family feel increasingly hopeless. Depression is common, as are anxiety syndromes. Children may develop school phobias, become withdrawn, cry or fight for no apparent reason, suffer nightmares, have separation anxieties, or find it difficult to concentrate on schoolwork.

Physicians who are not well-informed about the dynamics of chemical dependency may prescribe antianxiety drugs or antidepressants in response to such family problems. The use of these prescription medications, which dull perception of feelings, by a person in a family system that already discourages perception of feelings, usually does not improve the situation. Prescriptions of drugs like Valium or Xanax may also be given to a substance abuser, though this is dangerous both in terms of drug combinations (alcohol and Valium, for example) and the progression of chemical dependency.

Some individuals have a predisposition to mental health problems that is exacerbated by the use of alcohol or drugs. They may develop psychiatric problems of a severe nature that were not present, or were not severe, before chronic substance use.

Others with pre-existing mental illness may self-medicate with alcohol or illicit drugs. There are a number of reasons an individual may do this: traditional psychiatric medications may not have helped, the individual may dislike taking prescribed drugs because of unpleasant side effects or a distaste for the regimentation of regular medications, or the person may have never been properly diagnosed and treated for the mental illness.

Such people are described as "dual diagnosis" individuals. The presence of mental illness along with a chemical dependency complicates the treatment picture considerably. Few psychiatric specialists are fully familiar with the medical, psychological and spiritual issues of chemically dependent persons. Few substance abuse specialists are well-versed in the complex field of psychiatric assessment, diagnosis and treatment.

Dual diagnosis individuals make up a demanding treatment population—they present difficult circumstances, can be unpleasant and belligerent, and typically respond to treatment efforts slowly if at all. Many providers dislike working with dual diagnosis clients. The needs of the dual diagnosis individual are frequently overlooked, and the person is often lost in the cracks of the treatment and recovery system.

Spiritual. As people feel increasingly despondent about the family situation, their sense of meaning and purpose may be damaged or lost. They may lose all hope for improvement in the future. Often, people feel an immense anger at God, lose a faith they once had, or feel there is no reason to go on. They may have poor self-esteem and little sense of self-worth.

Parents may feel guilty for the chaos their children are exposed to in the drug- or alcohol-involved home. Biological mothers often feel guilty for the problems a child has due to prenatal drug effects. Without help or recovery, this guilt can fester and grow, becoming very destructive.

Young children who grow up in neighborhoods where drug dealing and violence are pervasive may never achieve a sense of hope, self-worth or personal efficacy. If their parents are users, if their family is disrupted, they may never have had the benefit of an environment where they could be presented with challenges and encouraged to struggle with them and find solutions.

Hopelessness and lack of personal efficacy may be the most serious consequences of a neighborhood drug trade and its accompanying violence. Children in this environment are especially vulnerable to becoming drug or alcohol dependent in the future. They have never learned that there are options other than drugs which help one cope with life's challenges and hardships

Family Treatment Increases Success

Research and clinical experience have both shown that when an individual is seeking treatment for chemical dependency, the likelihood of success is increased if the family is involved in treatment. Success in these efforts is absolutely in the best interests of children themselves—their lives will be better and richer if their families can be freed of the damaging effects of chemical dependency. Unfortunately, the structure of many treatment and recovery programs has made family involvement difficult.

Many programs are set up exclusively for men and cannot accept women. Others cannot work with couples—if one parent completes the program, he or she may return to a relationship with a partner who has not received treatment and is still actively using. Residential programs rarely include provisions for children; those that do have limited space, and a woman with more than one or two children may not be eligible for the program.

Some programs that claim to have "family treatment" offer counseling for adolescents but have no programs for younger children. Polydrug users have a difficult time finding programs that will accept them, as do individuals who have psychiatric illness in addition to a chemical dependency. (See Chapter 4 for a description of some of the limitations of treatment programs for mothers of young children or pregnant women.)

As individual providers, we can advocate for more and better treatment and recovery programs, especially ones that address the particular needs of the family. In planning our own programs, we can keep the needs of the family in mind. We must recognize that the family provides the greatest single influence on a child's overall development and well-being. No agency or provider can match the importance of the family in the child's physical, emotional, cognitive and social development.

Strategies for Working with Children Through Families

Some general suggestions for working with children from drug- and alcohol-involved families follow. The strategies described here could be applied in a number of different settings: health clinics, community centers, schools or churches, for example. The specific details may change, but the principles remain the same.

(Guidelines concerning the specific medical and developmental issues of prenatally exposed children are described in Chapters 6 and 7.)

Use a multidisciplinary team. One of the most essential strategies in working with children and families affected by drug- and alcohol dependencies is using a multidisciplinary team to provide a full range of services. The multidisciplinary team might include physician and nurse, psychologist, nutritionist, counselor, public health nurse, teacher and social worker. (See the table on the next page for a description of different members who might belong to a multidisciplinary team, and the role each fills in working with the family.)

There are several compelling reasons to work with a team of this nature.* Perhaps most obvious is the complexity of needs presented by the family affected by chemical dependency. No single provider—and usually no single agency—has the resources to address the full range of family needs.

Additionally, drug- and alcohol-involved families tend to distrust providers who represent authority or "the system." It may take several different providers to engage the family's trust, and the family may relate different parts of its history to different providers. Working together, a more comprehensive picture of the family situation can be gathered.

* The rationales included here for working with a multidisciplinary team are based substantially on material in Sokal-Gutierrez and others, work in progress, as are a number of the points in the next section.

Table 1

The Multidisciplinary Care Team

The multidisciplinary care team will vary from child to child, and from community to community, based on individual children's particular needs and the resources actually available in a community. Some teams will be small, consisting of two or three individuals; others may be large, consisting of many individuals and a number of agencies. The providers who might be included on a care team include:

- **Primary medical provider (physician, nurse practitioner or physician's assistant).** Sees child for well-checks and sick visits. Coordinates care with other medical specialists as necessary.

- **Public health nurse.** Carries out home visits to provide education and support. Assesses parent-child interactions and child's developmental performance in home setting.

- **Social services case manager.** Acts as a liaison between family and service agencies. Provides advocacy and assistance as necessary. Coordinates treatment plan and service provision across agencies

- **Drug or alcohol rehabilitation counselor.** Provides counseling and support during initial recovery/treatment period. Provides ongoing support as necessary at later periods.

- **Teacher.** Daycare, preschool or elementary school teachers provide information about child's learning and social behaviors and can provide further information about child's environment, strengths, limitations, typical daily routine, and so forth.

- **Nutritionist.** Assesses child's nutritional status. Provides education and counseling to caregiver about child nutrition. Develops diet plans for a child with special dietary needs.

(continued on next page)

Table 1
continued

- **Psychologist/Developmental specialist.** Provides testing and assessment of child's cognitive, motor, and adaptive development; temperament; and attachment behaviors. Makes recommendations for interventions to address areas of strength and weakness. Assists in development of treatment plan and academic Individualized Educational Program (IEP).

- **Physical therapist.** Provides therapy for physical problems having to do with range of motion, coordination, etc. Develops plan for family involvement, suggesting activities that will help child's motor development.

- **Masseur.** Provides massage to newborns and infants suffering effects of prenatal exposure to cocaine or other substances. Trains caregivers in therapeutic massage to stimulate child's neurologic development, if delayed, and acclimate child to human touch.

- **Learning specialist.** Assesses individual learning style, evaluating learning needs, and recommending appropriate academic program. Specifies remediation strategy when appropriate.

- **Psychotherapist or counselor.** Provides psychotherapeutic support to individual family members or family as a whole.

- **Health educator**. Educates caregivers about general and specific family health issues, such as HIV prevention, the importance of well-baby visits, family planning, and obstetrical and gynecologic care.

Finally, difficult legal and ethical issues often arise in working with drug-involved families. These might include questions about whether to report a family to Child Protective Services for suspected neglect or abuse, whether to recommend parental rights be terminated or reinstated, or whether to order "Do Not Resuscitate" for a terminally ill child with HIV. When considering such matters, it is advisable and helpful for different members of the team to discuss the full ramifications of any recommendations or decisions made.

Welcome the family. A treatment or service program seeking to help children from drug- and alcohol-involved families must provide a welcome to those families. The setting can be made interesting and inviting for family members. Ideally, family members could access or learn about services of interest to their individual needs: drug treatment, parent education, family planning or employment counseling. The environment should be physically comfortable and accessible for the families.

> "We didn't have a lot of money or resources for our 'Sanctuary Clinic,' so we couldn't provide extensive services to our families. But we offered a few options that were attractive to them.
>
> "Because we worked in a community where many parents do not have legal residency status, we set up our pediatric medical clinic in a church identified as a sanctuary church. Families knew they did not have to fear the Immigration and Naturalization Service when they came to see us. And the church was right in the neighborhood where most of the families lived, so it was easy for them to get to.
>
> "We set up each week in the old church gymnasium. We created a simple waiting area on one side of the gym by putting out a rug and some folding chairs and setting out a few toys. Most often, a mother or father bringing in a sick child will bring along the other children in the family. If we get three or four families out there at one time, we might have ten or fifteen kids in the waiting area. The parents talk with one another about their children, the kids play with one another and there's a nice sense of community.
>
> "We use a bilingual staff at the clinic because many of the families speak only Spanish, or are most comfortable speaking

> Spanish. Sometimes, we are able to have a nutritionist or a family planning counselor or an HIV educator come in. They talk with the families waiting for appointments. This has given us a remarkable opportunity to provide prevention and health education to people who don't often receive these services.
>
> "We always have all the children in the family come in and say 'hello' to the nurse or the doctor. The parent will bring in one child with a specific complaint, but may be most worried about the child without the appointment. They can mention their concerns without embarrassment while we're greeting the rest of the family. We can also learn a great deal about a child's home relationships by observing and getting acquainted with the siblings, and this has been very helpful with our prenatally-exposed kids."
>
> —Physician

Develop an alliance with the family. It is essential for providers to develop an alliance with the family, especially with the primary caregiver. Providers should emphasize the common goal shared with the family: the health and well being of the child (or children). Keeping this shared goal uppermost in discussions can help parents see providers as allies rather than as judgmental, punitive outsiders.

It is also useful to involve caregivers actively in assessment and planning. For example, providers can ask the caregiver about the child's activities, health and development. The importance of the family's role, and especially the caregiver's role, in the child's development can be stressed. Strengths in caretaking skills can be praised and reinforced.

Children's negative or difficult behaviors can be successfully reframed for the caregiver in many cases. For example, a child's "misbehavior" at bedtime might be seen as a call for a more structured environment. By helping the parent better understand what the child's behavior says, and supporting the parent's ability to deal with this situation in a positive way, the provider strengthens the sense of alliance with the family.

It is also important in encounters with the family to have some private time with the parent. This can allow the provider to assess the current status of the family in relation to substance use, family violence, and so forth. It is helpful to show this kind of individual attention to caregivers, validating that they and their concerns are also important. Providers may be able to offer support to a parent in recovery or treatment, or encouragement to a parent considering entering a recovery program.

Caring for families in a comprehensive way also provides direct and essential care for the individual child. Caregivers receiving this kind of ongoing support and education are more likely to provide good parenting overall. There is, in fact, some evidence that teaching caregivers certain specific skills in childrearing improves health outcomes such as growth and development, increases compliance with immunization schedules, and decreases rates of abuse, neglect, injuries and out-of-home placement (Dubowitz, 1989).

Set proper limits with the family and protect the child. Being an ally and a support for drug- and alcohol-involved families is not inconsistent with setting limits. Limit setting is an important strategy which, when used appropriately, contributes to the health of the family. Parents or other caregivers are often disorganized individuals who have difficulty keeping appointments, following through on instructions or acting responsibly with their children. Limit setting can assist such individuals in caring properly for their children. For families with young children, the most important limits have to do with protecting the welfare of the children.

In medical clinic settings, for example, providers caring for children must emphasize to caregivers the importance of regular medical follow-up. These regular visits are essential to allow providers to monitor the status of children with chronic problems and allow ongoing assessment of a child's general health: Does the child show any symptoms of neglect or abuse? Is she or he being properly nourished? Is she or he attending school regularly?

Teachers and counselors must also monitor children's health and school attendance. Where there is reasonable suspicion or proof that a child has been abused or neglected, a report will need to be made to Child Protective Services (CPS). Many providers may find it difficult to determine whether a suspicion is "reasonable," or a situation is reportable. Any member of the community can call CPS anonymously and speak directly with a caseworker. The CPS worker will be able to advise whether a given circumstance is reportable, and may help providers understand more about the likely dangers of a specific situation.

Parents and other caregivers should understand the value placed on school attendance and medical appointments, as well as the consequences they will face if their children stop attending school or if they miss appointments without calling the clinic and arranging for a new time.

People with chemical dependency are frightened when their disease becomes so overwhelming they are unable to care for their children or families. They may use denial to assure themselves that things are not so serious, and they may use more substance in an attempt to relieve themselves of their guilt and fear. But they do not like the ways substance use interferes with their ability to be good parents or caregivers.

> "I was working with a family where the children had been removed from the home because of drug-related neglect and abuse. Both parents had completed treatment programs and were at a court proceeding attempting to regain custody of their children. The judge indicated that he would need to see further evidence the home was a safe place before he would reinstate their parental rights.
>
> "The father became incredibly frustrated and angry at this, and shouted at the judge, 'I'm gonna kill you, man!'
>
> "So I got the father out of the courtroom and someplace I could talk to him privately, and I said, 'Hank, you can't go around threatening the judge like that. I know you're angry, but you will never get your kids back if you do this.' This man did not initially see that threatening to kill someone who had insulted him was not appropriate behavior here—in the neighborhood he came from, it would be expected. After we talked it over, he understood that the judge felt if Hank could threaten to kill him, he was probably also a danger to his children. When we went back to court, Hank apologized sincerely and made a genuinely favorable impression.
>
> "By taking his side on this, and explaining the social rules of the courtroom, I was able to maintain the family's trust. Seeing that I was committed to helping them get their kids back meant

> they listened more carefully when I worked with them on parenting skills. If I told them it wasn't appropriate to hit the baby with a belt, they believed me. They knew I cared about the children and the family. And I knew they really wanted to be good parents.
>
> "Eventually, the children were restored to the family, and the parents have done a pretty good job with them since then."
>
> —Child Protective Services caseworker

The provider setting limits is saying, "You and I both care about your children, and want to make sure they are safe. When your chemical dependency overwhelms you and your children are in danger, I will step in to make sure they are protected."

If children must be removed from their family's custody because of dangers in that setting, service providers must always work with the family towards reunification. This is a legal requirement. But more than this, the family is the best place for children to be. Providers must do whatever they can to strengthen the family's capabilities to care properly for children, and work consistently for reunification of children and caregivers whenever possible.

(See Chapter 6 for more specific assessment recommendations and further suggestions about limit setting and Child Protective Services.)

Help families maintain a sense of hope. Experience with individuals who have succeeded in recovery and treatment programs can offer providers the sense of hope they need to work successfully with drug- and alcohol-involved families. People in the most advanced stages of addiction, who were literally living in gutters, who were so physically addicted that they could barely stand long enough to spend their panhandling money on cheap wine or one more hit, have succeeded in achieving the miracle of recovery. To see this is truly remarkable and inspiring.

If you have not met individuals who have succeeded in long-term recovery, you may want to attend some open Alcoholics Anonymous or Narcotics Anonymous meetings in your area. These organizations are listed in the phone book. You might also speak with staff members at local recovery and treatment programs.

The model offered by individuals and families who have succeeded in recovery efforts can help providers maintain hope for the drug- and alcohol-involved families with whom they work. It is possible for the family's situation to improve, and it is even possible for the user to attain sobriety. Families coping with active chemical dependency are often not aware that others in similar situations have succeeded in recovery. If you can communicate this hope to families, consistently and positively, you can help pass along the ability to believe things could be better. From that bit of hope and faith, the willingness to embark on the path of recovery may appear and grow in a parent, a child or an entire family.

The Concept of Family Centers

Families affected by chemical dependency are often chaotic and dysfunctional, operating in a full-time crisis mode. In areas where whole neighborhoods are deeply affected by the drug epidemic, where violence is pervasive and helpful interventions difficult, the chaos may be even greater. Service providers working with such families know their needs may be considerable, and the provision of services challenging.

> "I spend an extraordinary amount of time just coordinating the services needed by one drug-involved family. It takes hours to call all the different agencies involved in care and support, arrange conferences, clear up confusion, make sure we're not duplicating services. Many of the families are very skilled at splitting off the providers, getting one agency angry at another, setting up fights between a therapist and a teacher. So we have to spend a lot of time being clear with one another and staying out of conflicts.
>
> "The families themselves get frustrated because so many different people are involved in their care, and they feel like they spend all their time traveling from one place to another just to get the help they need to survive. Then after spending all day going somewhere to see someone, they find out they're not getting what they needed in the first place.
>
> "Sometimes we talk about this dream of a multiservice

> center, where most services could be offered from a single location. It would be much easier for the families, and easier for the providers as well—we could follow up with one another if complications arose. And we could involve families more actively in planning coordinated support and care."
>
> —Social worker

Many policy planners and providers working with drug- or alcohol-involved families are advocating the development of family centers in areas with high levels of drug use and dependency. The family center would be a multiservice program for families affected by chemical dependency.

A broad range of services would be available in a single location. Services would be offered at reasonable hours for working parents, including early mornings, evenings and weekends, and would be free or low-cost, depending on ability to pay. Centers would be located in accessible areas, perhaps in community centers or other neighborhood facilities.

Outreach workers could canvass neighborhoods and enroll high-risk families in the center's support programs. Enrolled families would be offered a family assessment plan. The assessments would be repeated on a regular basis every six months. A case manager assigned to the family would help them plan their involvement in activities of interest, and could also coordinate the work of other community programs involved with the family.

Many families include members of the extended family and friends who have been "adopted" as family members. Program planning would include the needs of the entire extended family and provide programs of interest to all.

Services might include treatment and recovery programs, daycare for younger children, drop-in childcare for emergencies, therapeutic nursery programs for at-risk children (see Chapter 6 for a fuller description of therapeutic nurseries), GED programs for parents and teenagers, AA, NA, Al-Anon, other support groups, parent training groups, health care services, recreational activities, referrals for childcare services, emergency food and housing resources, employment counseling, and so forth. For families dealing with HIV or other life-threatening illness, there might be anticipatory grief groups, respite care or training on home care issues.

Programs could be offered to the general population as well. The centers could involve a broad range of organizations and agencies, including churches and community-based organizations. The centers would emphasize culturally sensitive services, using staff from ethnic and cultural backgrounds similar to those of the clients. Clients could comfortably use their native language, and programs would be geared to an educational level appropriate for the clients.

Today the family service center is still primarily a dream, but a number of programs are being set up that begin to meet these criteria. These programs all use a multidisciplinary team approach and are sensitive to the needs of underserved and culturally diverse populations. For example, Project STAR, a complete service program in Roxbury, Massachusetts, works with drug-involved families. The project provides evaluation and remediation programs for infants and toddlers, along with parenting skills workshops and drug treatment for caregivers. Families can live on-site during treatment and return for outpatient services upon discharge.

In San Francisco, the Department of Social Services has coordinated the work of approximately twenty agencies to provide a range of services to assist in the reunification of families involved in the foster care system. The Transitional Residential Infant Program can arrange services for children, caregivers and the extended family. Children may be referred, for example, for child assessment, developmental evaluation and therapeutic nursery programs.

Caregivers can participate in group and family therapy, are offered respite care in some cases, and receive the assistance of home health nursing if necessary. Parent education and parent treatment programs (including individual therapy and drug and alcohol programs) are also available. Extended family members can participate in groups for grandparents and other relatives.

These kinds of comprehensive service programs are intensive and somewhat costly, but the costs of ignoring chemical dependency, or of leaving things as they currently stand, is ultimately much higher. We hope to see more projects of this nature in the future.

❧ ❧ ❧

Amanda
An Infant and a Mother in Recovery

Amanda was born prematurely at 32 weeks gestation with classic, severe presentation of Fetal Alcohol Syndrome (FAS). She was the third child of her 35-year-old mother, Irene. Irene's other two children were in the custody of their father, and she was not in regular contact with them.

Irene, a large woman, had not realized she was pregnant for the first six months of her pregnancy. During that time she drank two 6-packs of beer a day. Once she realized she was pregnant, she cut back to three beers a day. She also smoked heavily, usually two packs of cigarettes daily. She denied use of other substances during the pregnancy, and the toxicology screen at time of delivery was negative. Because of Amanda's diagnosis of FAS, a report was made to Child Protective Services.

Amanda was small for her age—a little over two pounds at birth. She had the facial features often seen in children with FAS, including a flat nose, widely spaced eyes and a simple philtrum (i.e., the indented line between the nose and the lips was absent). Her fingers were short in proportion to her tiny hands, and her cry was high-pitched. Her blood sugar levels were dangerously low, and she needed to be monitored for hypoglycemia. She received glucose intravenously.

Amanda was placed in the hospital nursery so she could gain an adequate amount of weight. Irene visited her every day, spending most of her day at the hospital and eagerly participating in Amanda's feeding. She had been told that Amanda had FAS, but stated repeatedly that Amanda was a beautiful child who was developing normally. She resented any inference that Amanda might have future medical or developmental problems and became especially angry if anyone suggested her drinking or smoking had had any negative effects on Amanda.

Amanda fed reasonably well and was able to put on weight. At three weeks of age, she weighed about five pounds, and at that time was discharged and went home with her mother.

Follow-up: Amanda was followed weekly for six weeks for close monitoring of her weight gain. Irene brought her promptly to all of her appointments, and

Amanda was beautifully groomed and dressed at each visit. The mother continued to deny seeing any effects of FAS.

At each outpatient visit, a general screen for Amanda's developmental progression was completed. Amanda's milestones were generally about eight weeks late, but this was not surprising since she had been born six weeks premature. She was "floppy" and not very responsive at one month and smiled at about two months. It was not until three months that Amanda became genuinely interactive with others. Irene was thrilled at each new accomplishment and kept careful and meticulous records in Amanda's baby book.

Three months: At the visit when Amanda was three months old, Irene came in with alcohol on her breath. She was loud and boisterous at the clinic, overly familiar with patients and staff. She praised Amanda for learning to lift her head by herself, which she had done just that morning for the first time.

A drug and alcohol counselor was brought into the clinic to talk with Irene. The counselor confronted her about her drinking. Irene said she had cut down quite a bit during the pregnancy and immediately after Amanda's birth, but acknowledged tearfully that she was once again drinking heavily and felt out of control.

The counselor told Irene that her drinking was a health danger to herself and to Amanda. Irene agreed, and also agreed to meet with him, without drinking beforehand, the next day. Then the counselor arranged for a friend of Irene's to come to the clinic and give her and Amanda a ride home—the clinic could not allow Irene to drive Amanda home herself because she was intoxicated.

Irene and Amanda arrived for their appointment the next day. Irene again became very distraught, explaining to the counselor that she had tried unsuccessfully to stop drinking in the past. She had attended Alcoholics Anonymous meetings on and off for a year, and had failed in both an inpatient and an outpatient treatment program. She knew she was an alcoholic, but did not know what else to do. She was terrified that Amanda would be taken away from her now. "I have never been so desperate in my life. I would do anything possible to stop drinking," she said.

Irene agreed at this session to enter a recovery program for alcoholism if she could keep Amanda with her during her stay. The counselor made a number of calls that morning and was able to get Irene and Amanda on a waiting list for a local recovery program that accepted mothers with young children. Irene made a commitment to attend one Alcoholics Anonymous meeting a day while she was waiting to get into the recovery program, and the counselor reminded her that participation in AA required only that she have a desire to stop drinking.

For the next few weeks, Irene maintained frequent contact with the counselor and attended AA meetings regularly. She also drank on and off, usually binging when she did so, and was filled with remorse and shame afterwards. The counselor continued to acknowledge that Irene's motivation to stop drinking was greater than ever before, because it was tied into her desire to provide good parenting for Amanda.

Irene and Amanda were fortunate. An opening at the recovery program became available just before Amanda turned four months old.

Four months: At Amanda's four-month clinic visit, Irene proudly appeared one week clean and sober. Amanda was still very tiny and growing slowly, but she was feeding adequately, and her general health seemed fine except for her small size.

Amanda's head size was quite small. This is a typical feature of FAS and was a matter of concern to the medical staff. Small head size is strongly suggestive of mental retardation. While Amanda's gross motor milestones were within normal limits when corrected for gestational age, later milestones involving cognition and language probably would be delayed.

Irene did not ask about Amanda's developmental prognosis, but for the first time she also did not insist that Amanda was "a perfectly normal baby." Because Amanda's development was acceptable thus far, and because of the fragility of Irene's new sobriety, the staff decided to save a discussion of Amanda's potential developmental problems for a later visit. The continued love and care Irene showed Amanda was praised, and Irene was told, truthfully, that her sobriety would be a great benefit to her daughter's growth and well-being.

At the time of this writing, Amanda and her mother are still in the recovery home. Irene has been sober for nearly four weeks and is feeling hopeful about the future.

Comment: *Amanda is a child who has already been deeply affected by her mother's chemical dependency. Full Fetal Alcohol Syndrome (FAS) is prob-*

ably the only prenatal chemical exposure syndrome that has been described fully enough to allow providers to predict developmental outcome with some confidence. Because she has a small head, developmental delay and all of the standard features of FAS, Amanda will most likely be mentally retarded. She may have other kinds of learning and behavioral problems as well, including difficulties in concentration, retaining information or learning from past experience.

Amanda will do better, however, if she can grow up in a stable, consistent, loving home environment. Her mother's deep attachment and commitment may help this child cope more successfully with some of the challenges that lie ahead.

Irene's great love for Amanda may also be the final element she herself needs to succeed in achieving sobriety. Without this child in her life, she had little motivation to go through the suffering of early recovery, and she lacked commitment to the ongoing work her recovery would require. Her situation has changed, however, and her earlier failures in AA and the treatment programs do not necessarily mean she cannot succeed this time around.

The willingness of Amanda's pediatric medical providers to treat the family—to look after Irene's welfare as well as Amanda's—has given this family another chance for health and recovery. None of us can say for sure how things will go for Irene and Amanda, but today Irene is sober, and that is good for Amanda. This is an excellent example of how caring for the family contributes to the welfare of the child.

❧ ❧ ❧

Chapter 6

Prenatal to Preschool: The Developmental Picture

The impact of prenatal chemical exposure on a child's development depends on many different elements. These include the type or types of chemicals the mother used, the amount used, how often the substances were used, the point in fetal development during which they were used, and whether and what substances were combined (cocaine and alcohol, for example).

The child's development will also be affected by the family situation—does he or she have a family setting where it is possible to develop a solid emotional foundation and a sense of self-worth and value?

Each child has unique innate capabilities which also play a role in development. Children with similar prenatal exposure may have very different outcomes, and the reasons for the differences are not always clear.

In considering developmental issues for children with prenatal exposure, two essential points should be remembered:

1. **It is not possible to distinguish different drug and environmental effects clearly.** Pregnant women who use drugs frequently combine drugs as well. Crack cocaine users may drink alcohol and often also use marijuana. Drinkers usually smoke. Many people who use marijuana habitually also drink frequently. Most people who have chemical dependencies also have poor nutrition. Many chemically dependent women are living in poverty. There may be family violence or mental illness in the home of a substance abuser. Parents may be poorly skilled at rearing children. All of these factors influence the development of the fetus or child.
2. **We cannot know for certain a young child's developmental potential.** At the time a child with prenatal drug or alcohol exposure is born, and even during the first several years of life, we cannot determine developmental outcome with certainty. As the child grows and reaches school age, he or she may develop problems that were not originally anticipated. On the other hand, with appropriate early interventions and therapeutic work, children who appear at birth to have very poor prognoses may "catch up" a considerable amount and accomplish much more than was originally expected.

When working with drug or alcohol exposed children, providers must endeavor to understand the kinds of challenges the children are facing. Strategies should be planned that respond to these challenges and give children opportunities to improve or overcome their deficits. Most importantly, providers must maintain within themselves a belief that children with prenatal chemical exposure can be helped and deserve positive, appropriate care.

Issues During Pregnancy

Pregnant women who are deeply involved in the drug culture typically receive little or no prenatal care. A woman may be well into her pregnancy before she even realizes she is pregnant. For poor women especially, there may be no prenatal services available that are reasonably accessible, and/or she may be afraid of punitive consequences if she seeks medical care.

Among drug and alcohol dependent women, one or more of the following factors is likely to affect a pregnancy:

Poor nutrition. People using stimulants such as cocaine and amphetamines have little appetite. People using narcotics and alcohol often lose interest in food. The physical desire for food cannot compete with the physical desire for the substance, and where resources are limited they will always be spent on drugs or alcohol over food. Pregnant addicts/alcoholics tend to eat foods with little nutritious value and often eat very little at all. Weight gain throughout the pregnancy may be inadequate.

Polydrug use. Over the course of a pregnancy, a fetus may be exposed to a wide variety of substances, including cigarettes, marijuana, alcohol, cocaine, heroin, methadone, amphetamines and tranquilizers. While most users have a preferred substance, many will use other drugs if their preferred substance is not available. Cigarettes offer a "tonic" for the anxiety drug users often feel during periods between drug usage. Heavy smoking is common among drug users.

Depression and mental illness. Women caught in the cycle of addiction frequently experience significant depression with associated physical problems. Symptoms may include difficulty eating and sleeping, fatigue, inability to accomplish tasks, difficulty concentrating, and a general feeling of hopelessness and despair. It is difficult for a woman with significant depression to care adequately for herself or her pregnancy. Chemically dependent women may be experiencing other mental health problems as well. If women are prescribed antidepressants or antianxiety drugs, the developing fetus may suffer further effects from these medications.

Poverty. Chronic drug and alcohol use are often accompanied by financial difficulties, and many chemically dependent women are living in poverty. They have little money with which to care for themselves or their families. Their children need food, clothes, school supplies, spending money, etc. There is no money to pay for a babysitter to watch other children during prenatal visits; there is no money to pay for transportation to the clinic or medical office; there is no money to pay for vitamins or prescription medications recommended by a health care provider.

The already-burdensome needs of a family in poverty make it difficult to find resources to care for a pregnancy. Pregnant women living in deep poverty often feel that they have little or no power to change or improve their situations.

Undereducation. Women with chemical dependencies may also have limited educational background. Undereducation is inextricably linked to conditions of poverty. Like poverty, it can contribute to a sense of low self-worth and hopelessness. A lack of education will limit the success of a woman's efforts to end a dependency, move to a new neighborhood, get a job, and so forth. Women with limited education are also less likely to be knowledgeable about the benefits of prenatal care or about methods for accessing such care.

Violence. Chemically dependent pregnant women have greater exposure to violence than women who are not involved in addiction. Women in poverty, living in poor neighborhoods where drug trade is evident, cannot afford to move to a safer place. There are more frequent injuries to pregnant women in such neighborhoods from assaults, gunshots and general crime. Chemically dependent women may also be physically abused by their families, spouses or partners.

Poor maternal health. Maternal health may be compromised before a pregnancy by long-term drug or alcohol use, poor nutrition or medical conditions that have gone untreated (for example, sexually transmitted diseases, high blood pressure, tuberculosis or anemia). There is also an increased risk of HIV among women who use injection drugs themselves or are involved with a sexual partner who uses injection drugs. Women using crack cocaine or other smokable illicit substances are more likely to have had sexual contact with HIV carriers and are also at increased HIV risk.

Young mothers. Some of the women who use drugs and alcohol are teen mothers. These young women may have little or no experience caring for infants and often have few resources to turn to for advice or help. Parent training is especially important with teen parents.

While we tend to think of these problems as particular to impoverished women in inner-city neighborhoods, it is important to remember that similar problems face women in rural areas, and that many of these same problems affect middle and upper class women.

As we have mentioned earlier, one advantage middle and upper class women have is the greater availability of options—to seek medical care, to live in a "safe" neighborhood, to hire someone to help care for children or prepare family meals. But the problems of family violence, poor nutrition, depression, poor health and polydrug use are also common among addicted women who are not poor.

Any of these factors can have considerable impact on fetal development and pregnancy outcome. In combination, they represent a significant danger to a fetus. Common pregnancy complications for women who use drugs include:

- Low weight gain throughout the pregnancy.
- Placental abruption. (Placental abruption is the detachment of the placenta from the uterine wall. It is often seen in pregnancies affected by maternal cocaine use. With placental abruption, the fetus can lose its blood supply and may go into shock because of blood loss. The woman can also hemorrhage as a result.)
- Infectious diseases that can be passed to the fetus or newborn (herpes, chlamydia, syphilis, HIV, cytomegalovirus, toxoplasmosis, rubella, gonorrhea, group B streptococcal infection).
- Hypertension and tachycardia (high blood pressure and fast heart beat).
- Prematurity (sometimes up to three or four months).
- Precipitous delivery (one where labor comes on quickly and progresses to sudden delivery without moving through the usual phases).

(See Appendix B for information on the specific effects of various drugs on pregnancy outcome and fetal and child development.)

Issues in the Newborn Period

In the newborn period (the first month of life), a number of problems typically appear for the infant with drug or alcohol exposure. The following are some of the more common problems.

Prematurity. Prematurity is the single most common difficulty for newborns with chemical exposure. Along with prematurity come a host of related problems: low birth weight, feeding problems (children may need to be tube fed), respiratory distress and inadequate development of the lungs (children may require a ventilator), and small head size (usually associated with developmental delay).

Neurologic problems. A variety of neurologic problems may appear in the newborn period. Children may suffer strokes, seizures, blindness, deafness and hypertonicity (rigidity in muscles). Many children have an unusually high-pitched cry, which is a sign of neurologic damage.

Withdrawal problems. Newborns exposed to addictive drugs, such as heroin, alcohol, amphetamines or cocaine, may need medical management of withdrawal complications. Withdrawal for the newborn can be life-threatening. Physical and neurologic symptoms of withdrawal may last several weeks. Common symptoms of withdrawal include irritability, persistent and inconsolable crying, jerkiness and rigidity, seizures, sleep disturbances and feeding problems.

Increased risk of Sudden Infant Death Syndrome (SIDS). Children born after exposure to methadone and heroin have an increased risk of SIDS. There have been mixed reports on the rate of SIDS among infants exposed prenatally to cocaine, but at present these infants do not appear to have an increased risk over infants without prenatal chemical exposure.

Developmental problems. Children with substance exposure may have a number of developmental problems. Their milestones may be delayed; they may not respond to their environment in the same ways as other children; and their social relationships with family members may be difficult.

Table 2

Normal Development Milestones

birth	Responds to sounds (rattle, bell). Looks briefly at moving objects. When lying on stomach, moves head to side.
1 month	Can hold head up a few seconds. Follows moving objects part way. Responds to speech. Begins vocalizing (coos, gurgles, grunts). Looks directly at caregiver's face.
3 months	Pushes up on forearms when placed on stomach.
4 months	Holds head balanced. Follows slowly moving objects well. Laughs. Sustains vocalizations (cooing, gurgling). Has spontaneous social smile. Shows awareness of strange situations.
6 months	Rolls over back to front. Sits, leaning forward on hands. Bounces when placed in standing position. Grasps toys. Shakes rattle. Transfers toys from one hand to another. Makes vowel sounds ("ah, ah").
8 months	Crawls on belly.
9 months	Pulls to a stand. Sits without support. Bangs two objects together. Responds to name. Responds to social play (pat-a-cake, peek-a-boo). Holds own bottle. Feeds self a cracker.

(continued on next page)

Table 2
continued

11 months	Cruises (walks holding on with two hands).
1 year	Walks holding on with one hand. Stands alone briefly. Builds tower of two blocks. Plays ball.
15 months	Walks well. Stops and starts with control. Says three to five words. Points or vocalizes when wants something.
18 months	Walks fast. Runs stiffly. Builds tower of three or four blocks. Says ten words. Says own name. Feeds self (but spills food). Has a special toy (blanket, doll).
2 years	Runs well. Kicks large ball. Walks up and down stairs with rail (two feet on each step). Builds tower of six or seven blocks. Uses three-word sentences. Puts on simple garment. Calls self by name.
3 years	Rides tricycle. Climbs stairs, alternating feet. Jumps from higher to lower area. Builds tower of nine or ten blocks. Knows own sex. Feeds self well. Puts on shoes. Unbuttons clothing.
4 years	Walks downstairs, alternating feet. Hops. Repeats four numbers. Brushes teeth. Plays cooperatively with other children.
5 years	Skips, using feet alternately. Draws recognizable person. Names primary colors. Dresses and undresses self.

Training Parents and Caregivers

"I went to see my new grandson when he was four weeks old. He had just come home from the hospital because he was born prematurely. I knew he would be little, but I was shocked at what he looked like and how he acted.

"He was jumpy, he cried all the time, and all of a sudden he would close up his eyes and get real stiff all over. We would feed him a little formula and he would just spit it all right back up. I told my daughter she needed some help learning how to hold that baby.

"I picked him up and smiled right at him. I held him out in front of me and bounced him up and down very gently. He just screamed and cried. I pulled him in close and looked him in the eye and sang him my favorite lullaby. He stretched his little body away from me and screamed again.

"I don't understand this. I have handled a lot of children and grandbabies in my time, and I've never had a child act like this. He seems so unhappy all the time. I don't know how he can feel this, but I think he hates me.

"What can I do to help? I can't imagine how to begin to love this child."

—Grandmother

Infants with chemical exposure may continue to have a variety of problems as they grow and develop. They may require special attention in many areas. Such children present a considerable challenge to parents and caregivers. Actions as simple as picking the baby up, changing diapers, feeding, or putting it down to sleep, can become major ordeals.

Often babies with this kind of irritability are showing signs of overstimulation. Their nervous systems have not developed as fully or in the same manner as children without chemical exposure. The stimulation of their environment is far too powerful; they are raw and sensitive, and they do not know how to screen out all the painful distractions.

A "normal" baby can be gently bounced while a grandmother smiles and coos at it. The baby will look at the grandmother's face, seem fascinated and involved, and around age two weeks may even start smiling in response to her loving attentions.

For a chemically exposed child, this may be too many things at one time. He is held dangling out in front of his grandmother and the lack of "boundaries" around him is frightening. She bounces him gently and the sensation is painfully irritating. She looks into his eyes and he cannot make sense of the visual patterns in front of him. He screams, becomes rigid, closes his eyes and turns away from her.

One of the most important interventions for infants with chemical exposure is careful training of caregivers. Caregivers need to know what to expect from the child, how to read his or her signals, and how best to respond. By carefully attending to their child's signals, they can help the neurologically immature child become more tolerant of a variety of stimulation (touch, vocalization, visual stimuli). This can help the child respond more comfortably to the family environment and provide reinforcement for the parent who might otherwise feel rejected by the baby's behavior.

Parents need validation for the good work they do with the child and reassurance that the child depends on and appreciates the care they give. They need help gaining realistic expectations of what this child's role will be in their lives. Many new mothers bring their own needs to the parent/child relationship and these may not be realistic. Mothers with backgrounds of poverty, violence, addiction and low self-esteem are especially likely to expect the baby to "heal me and love me and fill all my needs."

Social and Emotional Development

> "Many times in my work, I've seen medical providers assess prenatally exposed kids and find they aren't attaining milestones at the expected rate. The children are diagnosed as having cognitive deficits, and that becomes the primary focus of treatment. But, in fact, the cognitive deficit is often secondary to the emotional problems the children are facing. They have troubled parents who cannot provide the secure attach-

> ment base the children need to develop cognitively. The doctors are treating the children's slowed development, when the real focus of treatment should be the troubled family and how to improve these children's emotional health and safety."
>
> —Physician

Developmental theorists have emphasized the importance of an infant's ability to attach to the mother or another primary caregiver. Some have suggested that this attachment behavior is an inherited characteristic of the human species, necessary for survival. The relationship of the child to his or her primary caregiver in the first year of life will result in patterns of behavior that influence emotional, social and intellectual capabilities in later life. Children who have not had successful attachments may have difficulties sharing, playing with other children and reading social cues appropriately.

Patterns of Attachment Behavior

Mary Ainsworth, a researcher in child development interested in learning more about the attachment behaviors of infants and toddlers, developed a research assessment tool called the "strange situation" (Ainsworth, 1973). In this setting, a baby is brought by its mother into an unfamiliar room. The mother has been coached ahead of time about what she is to do and how she is to act.

Once the baby is comfortable, a stranger enters, spending some time with the mother and baby. Then the mother leaves the room, returning a few minutes later. This sequence is repeated several times, and the child's responses to the mother and the stranger are observed.

Using this instrument, Ainsworth and her associates identified different types of attachment behaviors. These behaviors were organized by the children into patterns that influenced their social and emotional lives. The child who could rely on and trust the caregiver's presence was also able to explore the "strange situation" and tolerate the appearance of a stranger. The child could interact with the stranger with minimal anxiety, seeming secure that the caregiver would return if needed. This child is said to have a *secure* pattern of organization.

Other children were less able to trust their caregiver, and in fact put considerable effort into monitoring the caregiver's whereabouts and actions. They were less able to explore the newness of the strange situation and less willing to interact with the stranger. Their caregivers tended to be ambivalent and unreliable. The children themselves tended to use ambivalent or avoidant behaviors to gain attention from the caregiver. These children have *insecure* patterns of organization.

A third type of organization pattern was also described in the Ainsworth studies. These children had caregivers similar to those of the insecure children, but had not developed an organized response (ambivalence or avoidance, for example). They are said to have *disorganized* attachments. In the absence of their caregiver, they might cry, withdraw, cling to someone or something, yell, get fussy, break or hit toys, bite or just sit still. Unlike the other children, there is no consistent pattern to their attention-seeking or attachment behaviors.

Recently, other researchers have used the Ainsworth instrument to compare children with drug exposure to a group of children without exposure (Howard, Rodning & Kropenske, 1989). All the children had been born prematurely at the same gestational age. Among these 18 month olds, the children born drug exposed had average scores on the assessment and were not significantly more insecure than the comparison group. However, the children's patterns of behavior were unusual compared to children without drug exposure.

For example, their response to new toys and the departure of their caregivers did not bring forth the strong feelings and reactions often observed when using this assessment tool. Their behavior during unstructured play situations was also unusual—they were more likely to scatter or hit toys, and less likely to play with them in any representational way. And the majority of the children who did have insecure attachments also had disorganized attachments.

These studies suggest that the initial physiologic effects of prenatal chemical exposure may reach into other areas of development as well. The toddlers were affected in the ways they expressed their feelings, their ability to establish and organize important relationships, and the way they thought about toys and play. Emotional, social and cognitive development all appeared to be affected by their prenatal drug exposure.

A Word of Caution

As you hear about such studies you may see a controversy developing between two "camps" with different theories about prenatal drug and alcohol exposure. The first includes researchers who study and emphasize the biochemical or physiologic effects. They are likely to find compelling physiologic consequences of prenatal exposure to drugs.

The second includes researchers who emphasize environmental or psychologic effects. Their studies are likely to confirm the impact of poverty, violence, parental abandonment or other difficult family dynamics on a child's development.

We must remember to evaluate these studies carefully. The study cited above describes behaviors reported anecdotally by many providers working with children with substance exposure, so it "makes sense" when you hear about it. However, it involved only 18 infants born drug exposed overall, and, like many studies of this nature, has been criticized for some of its methodological weaknesses.

This does not necessarily mean the study is invalid. But it reminds us of something we already know: we must see many more carefully designed studies of many more children before we can speak confidently about the extent and origin of deficits related to prenatal drug exposure. This "nature vs. nurture" debate is certain to continue for many years to come.

Meanwhile, for front-line providers, the ideas developed by Mary Ainsworth continue to be useful. At an early age, children learn ways of organizing their relationships and behavior that will influence their entire lives. To the extent that we can help them develop successful attachments—to caregivers and family members, to peers, and to others—we are also helping to lay a foundation for other essential competencies now and in the future.

It is not that important for a provider to know whether a toddler's aggressiveness developed in response to prenatal drug exposure or to uneven parenting in a series of foster homes. The responses we are able to offer are the same: to support consistent and loving care in the home, to provide consistent and appropriate care in our own setting, and to identify and emphasize each child's individual strengths. These interventions will be useful for any child, no matter what his or her particular issues may be.

Therapeutic Nursery Programs

Therapeutic nursery programs are being used in some areas to respond to the particular needs of children at risk. "At risk" is a deliberately vague term used to refer to children at increased risk for physical injury, emotional difficulties, developmental delay or learning problems.

Among those most likely to be at risk are children from drug- or alcohol-involved families; children with prenatal chemical exposure; children from homes where there is domestic violence; children who have been placed in a number of different foster settings; children of poverty; and medically fragile children (children with life-threatening or other severe medical conditions).

The therapeutic nursery recognizes that children with these difficult histories, many living in chaotic or dysfunctional families, will face particular challenges developing the social, academic and emotional skills necessary to succeed in school and society.

They may have neurologic or developmental deficits that make learning difficult. Their families may have been unable to provide them with the consistency, role models and sense of personal identity that allow a child to develop a positive sense of self-worth. If their families are quite disorganized, the children may be unable to develop an understanding of causal relationships—"If I do A, then B will happen;" or, "If I want X to happen, I can help that along by doing Y and Z."

Staff in the therapeutic nursery setting are specially trained in observation and assessment. They are able to evaluate a child's behavior and select the appropriate therapeutic response to help the child develop needed skills and capabilities. Staff can evaluate whether a child is responding to too much or too little stimulation in a given situation.

A child with poor impulse control and sudden bursts of aggressive behavior (hitting or biting other children, for example) will be helped to increase his or her ability to control anger and express it in a more appropriate fashion. A child who is withdrawn and has a difficult time with attachments will be allowed, slowly and carefully, to develop greater tolerance for small group activities with other children.

The child/staff ratio in the therapeutic nursery setting must be kept very low for the program to succeed. Children appropriate for such programs need considerable individual attention and generally do not share attention well. By receiving intensive individual time with staff, a child is less compelled to engage in problematic behaviors to attract the attention he or she wants and needs (aggressive behaviors, throwing tantrums, destroying toys, etc.) In some situations, the ratio of children to staff may need to be as low as two or three to one.

While the therapeutic nursery cannot take the place of the family in importance, it can mediate some of the attachment difficulties the child may face at home. The staff can provide a consistent, caring presence for the child. A child who cannot trust his mother to be available because of her drug or alcohol dependence may be able to place that trust in a nursery teacher. This early ability to trust another human being is essential to healthy development.

Working with Parents

The therapeutic nursery cannot operate successfully without also taking into consideration the needs of the child's parents. This is another area which distinguishes the therapeutic nursery from the usual community daycare or nursery programs. For example, the program must be physically located near the families it seeks to serve. Scheduling must be flexible to some extent: the parents of at-risk children are often disorganized, and are not able to abide by strict drop-off and pick-up times. Dietary guidelines that may be set forth in community daycare ("no sugar in the morning; no food after 9:00 a.m.") are unlikely to be followed by these parents. While staff will want to establish guidelines and set limits with parents, this must be done in a patient, non-punitive manner.

The therapeutic nursery program must also establish a sense of collaboration with parents and family. Parent training programs should be offered on a regular basis. In some cases, the nursery can be co-located with a drug treatment or alcohol recovery facility. While the parent is attending support groups and individual counseling, the child is cared for at the nursery.

The parent may actually participate in the nursery as a regular part of the daily schedule, learning from the staff how to care for his or her child, what the child is saying by various behaviors, and how best to respond. As the parent-child pair experience successes, the essential base of emotional attachment between the two can begin to build and solidify.

Some Results and Recommendations

> "Head Start programs have been wonderful supports in the lives of many children, and the concept of giving at-risk kids a 'head start' has been a useful one. But children who have been chemically exposed need much more than this. I can't get my patients into Head Start programs until they are three years old, and that's way too long for these children to wait. I like to think of the therapeutic programs for kids with chemical exposure as 'Jump Start' programs. Because of the range of neurologic, cognitive, physical and emotional challenges they face, they really need help getting going right away. If we don't intervene early, we may lose our capability to 'get them going' at all."
>
> —Physician

Head Start and other community daycare programs can be considered "enrichment" programs, which are of tremendous value to many children. The child born chemically exposed, however, often needs more than enrichment. The child may require a therapeutic program capable of responding to the developmental demands faced by such children and aware of the difficulties faced by children living in drug- or alcohol-involved families.

A child with substance exposure needs a program that can tolerate and adapt to the possible disorganization and chaos of the parents. He or she needs a program that will put an extraordinary effort into maintaining a relationship with the family, so the child can continue to benefit from the program. Standard community daycare programs do not have the resources for such intensive work, and engaging drug- and alcohol-involved families in those programs may be too disruptive for the other families participating.

Therapeutic nursery programs are not new in concept. They have been utilized for over 25 years in work with children who have special emotional or developmental needs. In the past, therapeutic nurseries have often been located in child guidance centers, and some have had a strong psychiatric focus.

The therapeutic nursery today, using a multidisciplinary team to respond to the needs of the child and support the strengths of the family, is a concept well worth supporting. As we see children facing increasing challenges in their families and neighborhoods, at ever earlier ages, programs of this type have the potential to assist in powerful ways.

Researchers are now beginning to design well-controlled studies to measure the levels of improvement in children who participate in the programs, and to determine which intervention programs are most effective. Most of the information concerning improvement comes from anecdotal experiences thus far, yet reports from these programs are encouraging.

The Salvin Special Education Center in Los Angeles works with children ages three to five who have experienced prenatal exposure to drugs. Approximately half of their students have been able to transfer to regular school classes, with the ongoing assistance of special tutoring and counseling.

The Chicago-based NAPARE group (National Association for Perinatal Addiction Research and Education) has followed 300 babies exposed to cocaine before birth who have received intensive interventions. Looking at ninety of the children when they reached the age of three, they found that 90 percent demonstrated normal intelligence, 70 percent had no significant behavioral problems and 60 percent did not require speech therapy.

New York City also has a special education preschool program for children at risk for developmental difficulties. Discussions with preschool teachers in these settings indicate that many of the children who receive intensive services gain skills and catch up in areas that were known to be weak at the outset. These New York preschool programs include group activities where caregivers receive parent education, learn about their individual child's development, and are given instruction on how to support their child's learning needs in the home. The children who are receiving this combination of school and home-based developmental services are showing the most improvement.

The recommendation to develop and utilize therapeutic nursery programs for children with prenatal drug and alcohol exposure is not without controversy. The most heated point of debate is whether we do more harm than good by "tracking" or labeling these children at an early age. In many cases, it is true that children who are expected to do poorly in a public school setting *will* do poorly even if they are capable of doing better. (See Chapter 8 for more on the issue of labeling, and Chapter 9 for a related discussion of children's different approaches to learning.) And, certainly, with all we have heard thus far about the deficits of children exposed to drugs and alcohol, it would be only natural to wonder if a student with a history of drug exposure would be able to succeed in the classroom.

It is essential that therapeutic nursery programs be properly administered and managed to deal with the problems of labeling. The services offered in a therapeutic nursery setting would be useful to *any* child, at risk or otherwise, but should be utilized primarily for children who are severely affected by prenatal chemical exposure—a small percentage of the overall population of children with substance exposure.

Because we see indications that early and aggressive interventions through the therapeutic nursery milieu help many of these children catch up on development and skills, we believe such programs are necessary. This kind of experience maximizes the child's chances of being integrated into a regular school program by kindergarten or first grade. It is with this goal in mind that therapeutic programs are recommended at early ages for children who experience considerable effects of prenatal drug or alcohol exposure.

❧ ❧ ❧

James
A Preschooler in a Therapeutic Nursery

Aurora, a three week old, came to the clinic for follow-up after premature birth and prenatal crack cocaine exposure. Her mother, Cassandra, had entered a treatment program and was given custody of the baby. At the clinic visit, Cassandra seemed to be drug free, attentive and genuinely concerned with her baby's well-being. The staff described some of the problems babies exposed to cocaine tend to have, and helped Cassandra prepare for the challenges of caring for Aurora.

As the visit came to a close, Cassandra asked if the doctors could also see her son James. She worried that he, too, might have suffered from prenatal cocaine exposure. She had used crack during her pregnancy with James, and as a newborn he had behaved much like Aurora. Now that he was three, he was becoming increasingly hard to manage. She was unable to get him to sit still or listen to her. She had tried yelling, spanking and threatening him, but he still did just as he pleased. She also worried about his speech. "This child talks plenty, but I do not understand what he is saying most of the time."

James had received sporadic medical care during his life and had had some of his vaccinations. He lived at home with his mother, grandmother and uncle. He was not enrolled in a daycare program and did not often have an opportunity to socialize with other children. He spent most of his day in the apartment, watching television with Cassandra.

James was invited into the exam room. He was an active, jittery boy who walked well and seemed coordinated for his age. He appeared physically healthy. As the physician approached him, James jumped back and screamed. He turned to his mother. "Go on, see the doctor," she shouted, pushing him away. "You embarrass me." She attended to Aurora, and James, standing alone in the middle of the room, took on a scowl of fury.

James' speech was markedly delayed. Over the course of the visit, he babbled like a much younger child. He said a few words, including "mama," "stop," "no," "James," "Sam" (his uncle) and "truck." He had some of the typical speech problems of younger children—confusing "R's" for "W's" and lisping slightly. Of greater concern was his inability to form simple sentences and his continuing use of babbling. His mother was unable to understand him because he was not speaking actual words.

James was also noted to have problems with asthma. Cassandra indicated that he had been diagnosed at a previous doctor's visit, but she had not pursued further care or treatment. She had been told by a friend that asthma medicine would make James more active, and she felt she could not handle him if that were the case. He had suffered a few episodes of breathing difficulty, but his mother said it did not seem all that serious and it did tend to quiet him down.

Medication was prescribed for James's asthma, and the importance of regular medical care for his condition was emphasized to Cassandra. She was also told what to watch for to determine whether James was ever in an acute crisis with his asthma. She was advised to keep the home as free of dust and irritants as possible and agreed that the family's pet cat could be moved outside.

James received his pending vaccinations, was referred for speech and hearing evaluation, and was set up on a six-month schedule of well-child visits. The physician also offered to try to enroll James in a daycare program, and Cassandra willingly agreed if such a program would not cost her money and would give her a break from James on occasion.

Throughout the visit, James wandered about the exam room, touching equipment, knocking things over, stamping his foot and screaming. At each new distraction, Cassandra would shout at him, hit him lightly, or pointedly ignore him and look at the baby.

Follow-up: James' hearing tested normally. With the assistance of the medical clinic, he was able to enroll in a special research program at a local university for children with drug exposure. Through the program, James received regular speech therapy as well as therapeutic nursery services. Transportation to and from the nursery was provided, and James spent four to six hours a day there. Cassandra was also involved in a parent training class through the university program, which she attended intermittently.

James responded well to the nursery setting and speech therapy. Over the next couple of years, his ability to attend to tasks improved, he began to solve simple puzzles, and his speech and language skills slowly caught up to age-appropriate levels. When he came in for his well-child visits, he interacted with clinic staff in a more friendly manner. As his speech improved, he told them about his school and the other children there. Cassandra continued to shout at him often, but the two also showed some affection. He enjoyed his younger sister.

When James was five, he was enrolled in a regular kindergarten class at the local public school. He was not identified to the school as a child with drug exposure. He got along well with his classmates and his speech was understandable to all. James frequently became angry at his teacher, however, and disrupted the class often by shouting and throwing tantrums. His teacher, in a discussion with James' pediatrician, complained that the boy's mother did not seemed concerned that James had these problems and had failed to show up for two parent-teacher conferences.

Because James continued to disrupt the class, his teacher requested an Individualized Education Program (IEP) meeting. This was arranged, and was attended by his teacher, his mother, the school principal, and the school psychologist. As a result of the IEP, James was referred for mental health services at a nearby community mental health center. He participated in a weekly play therapy group there, where he worked on social skills and impulse control.

James's impulse control did improve somewhat, but at the end of the year he was still considered a "problem student" by his teacher. His learning skills were adequate, however, and he was promoted to first grade. He would continue to participate in his weekly play therapy group over the summer and would be enrolled in a regular first grade class when school started again.

***Comment:** James was able to benefit considerably from participation in a therapeutic nursery program. It is certainly questionable whether he would have succeeded in his kindergarten year without the help he gained from his nursery program and speech therapy.*

James' relationship with his mother is somewhat difficult. Her manner with him is abrupt and rough at times. She criticizes him frequently, hits him occasionally (though not abusively to anyone's knowledge), and fails to show up at school conferences.

However, the affection and caring between mother and son has also been demonstrated to providers. Within his family, James is receiving the attention and sense of belonging he needs to develop well. Many of the children we work with have caregivers who do not have optimal parenting skills. In most of these instances, however, the children are still in the optimal home setting—a place where they know they belong.

James' school career is uncertain at this point in the story. His kindergarten teacher had difficulty with him, and did not seem especially well-connected to the boy. If he is able to establish a more positive relationship with his first grade teacher, his performance may improve. On the other hand, it is also possible that James will continue to have behavioral problems, and that he would benefit from an ongoing program of counseling and therapeutic support outside the classroom. Repeated assessments of his progress will be essential in the future.

❧ ❧ ❧

Jamika
A Normal Toddler

Jamika was 15 months old the first time her father brought her to the medical clinic. She came in at the recommendation of the family's social worker for a well-baby visit and measles vaccination. Jamika had recently arrived in town from a neighboring county, so her father did not have her medical and birth records.

Jamika's father, Jackson, had three other children by the same mother (ages eight, six and four). Both he and his wife had a history of drug use, but Jackson had entered a treatment program a few years earlier and had been clean and sober for three years. Two years ago he had moved north and separated from his wife, bringing the three children with him.

Jamika's mother had been arrested on burglary and drug possession charges and was in jail at the time of Jamika's birth. In the months prior to her incarceration, Jackson suspected she had been using heroin and crack cocaine. He did not know what, if any, substances she might have used while in jail. Jamika was put in foster care after birth, and Jackson obtained custody when she was 13 months old.

On examination, Jamika appeared to be a healthy and happy child. Jackson believed she was adjusting well to her new family, and her siblings were quite excited to have a new little sister. Jamika was cheerful, energetic, walked well and said several words. She was shy on first meeting the doctor and nurse, but warmed up quickly and was very engaging when she did. On developmental assessment, she was at normal levels for her age on all measures.

Jackson was concerned about Jamika's health and hoped to learn from this visit whether her suspected drug exposure would affect her development in any way. His other children, who were seen by another pediatrician, were all doing well, though the oldest was having some difficulties with reading.

The doctor explained that Jamika's prognosis was unclear, especially in the absence of medical records that could provide information about prenatal exposures she might have had. Because Jamika's mother was known to have used injection drugs and crack cocaine, however, the risk of HIV (infection with the virus which causes AIDS) was discussed with Jackson. He agreed to have Jamika tested for HIV, and blood was drawn for that purpose. Medical and birth records were ordered from Jamika's old home town.

Follow-up: Jamika and her father returned in two weeks for follow-up and results of the HIV antibody test. The test results were negative, indicating that she was not infected with HIV. She was given her measles vaccination. Though her next well-baby visit would typically be at 18 months, the doctor scheduled a visit in four weeks, expecting by that time to have earlier medical records on Jamika.

At this second follow-up appointment, the records had arrived and the doctor discussed them with Jackson. They indicated that Jamika's mother used heroin early in the pregnancy. She was incarcerated at four months' gestation and was placed on methadone maintenance while in jail. Jamika was a two kilo (four-and-a-half pound), full-term baby, who experienced moderate withdrawal from methadone for about ten days after birth. During this period, she was jittery, vomited frequently, suffered diarrhea and some loss of weight, and showed an exaggerated startle reflex. She was released to foster care once the symptoms of withdrawal had subsided and she was again gaining weight.

Medical records during her first year of life indicated that her developmental milestones occurred at normal times, and that she was a pleasant and well-liked child.

Because Jamika's appearance continued to be excellent, her social skills considerable, and her development within normal limits, she was placed on a regular schedule for well-baby visits without further special follow-up. At three years of age, her development continued to be within normal limits. In the future, the father was advised to monitor Jamika's school performance in the same way he had his other children's, and to feel free to discuss any questions about Jamika's health or development with the clinic staff.

Comment: *Jamika's story offers a happy example of a child who experienced prenatal chemical exposure but appears, so far, to be developing in excellent physical, cognitive and emotional health. It is not clear why some children do so well and others do poorly after similar exposures.*

Jamika's physician evaluated her patient as an individual child with a history of, among other things, prenatal drug exposure. Though she was aware of the possibility that Jamika might have physical or cognitive problems related to her prenatal experiences, she did not assume that to be the case. By looking at Jamika's unique situation and capabilities, she was able to provide the most useful evaluation for the family and the child.

❧ ❧ ❧

Chapter 7

Taking Care of Infants and Toddlers

For the caregivers of some children with drug or alcohol exposure, simple daily tasks such as feeding, holding and diapering can be very challenging. Many of the children are easily overstimulated, and usual methods of care will not be successful. Providers working with young children (below school age) can learn some simple techniques which will make these tasks easier, and can teach these skills to parents and other caregivers.

In this chapter, straightforward suggestions in these areas are offered, along with guidelines for developmental assessment and a schedule of medical care.

Medical Care

As we have mentioned previously, the needs of any particular child or family must be individually considered. In general, children who have experienced prenatal drug or alcohol exposure will be served best by more frequent medical care than other children. They may also require attention to some details that would be less important for their non-affected peers. The following schedule of medical visits provides a general guideline for frequency and focus of visits for children with alcohol and drug exposure.

Prenatal care. Regular obstetrical visits are critical to the well-being of the fetus and mother. The obstetrician, family practitioner or nurse midwife starts the process of preventive care. A prenatal visit to the pediatrician is highly recommended. This can help establish trust, provide education about the schedule of well-baby visits, and address some of the mother's concerns about her baby's health. Women who are using drugs or alcohol can be assisted into recovery or provided counseling.

Labor and delivery. Labor and delivery need to be closely monitored by the perinatal team (obstetrician, neonatologist, pediatrician). Complications are common among mothers who use drugs and alcohol. Where there are signs and symptoms of substance use, toxicology screens are often completed on mother and infant. The perinatal team will identify any drug present that might endanger the infant's health and plan interventions necessary to protect the child from drug effects or withdrawal problems.

In-hospital neonatal care. While the child is still in the hospital, the perinatal team should complete assessment and management of drug effects and other perinatal complications. If the infant goes into the Intensive Care

Unit (ICU) because of prematurity or withdrawal, hospital staff should provide nurturing physical contact for the child as much as possible. Family support and contact should also be facilitated. It is important to avoid blaming the mother or family for the child's problems. Strong bonding between family and child is essential for the child's current and future well-being, and this is difficult if a family feels judged or blamed by hospital staff.

Discharge plan. The discharge plan is made by the hospital's social services unit, with input from the child's health care team. The plan should include the current condition, special care needs, and placement of the child (see the section on out of home placement). The first well-baby follow-up visit will be scheduled. Family assessment is also important. What does the family need to know to care properly for the baby? Are any supplies needed by the family (diapers, formula, car seat)? Will mother and child be assigned to a recovery program? Is there a program that will accept them?

Standard care issues that should be covered with the family include feeding, sleeping, diaper changing, dressing, caring for umbilical cord and circumcision, car seat safety, symptoms of illness, taking the child's temperature, and the well-baby appointment.

Special care needs that may need to be covered include educating the family about drug effects and withdrawal, how to calm and feed the baby, use of special medications or care equipment (such as sleep monitors), emergency measures (CPR, or how to check the baby's vital signs), and follow-up appointments.

Families without experience caring for newborns may need the assistance of a public health nurse who can visit the family frequently (every day or two) in the first week or two after birth.

Well-baby visits. Standard schedules of periodic well-baby visits have been established by the American Academy of Pediatrics as well as by federal and state programs. The scheduled visits take place at two weeks, then at two, four, six, nine, twelve, fifteen, eighteen and twenty-four months of age. For children with prenatal chemical exposure, more frequent visits are recommended. For children with low birth weights, weekly visits may be necessary to monitor weight gain in the first months of life.

After 24 months, the standard schedule for well-baby visits is every one to three years. For children with chemical exposure, more frequent visits are recommended. Providers should assess the child's status and make appropriate recommendations to the family.

First well-baby visit. At this visit, a thorough medical history of the child is obtained, using hospital records and the family's report. Particular attention should be paid to complications in the prenatal period, birth and delivery, and postnatal course. Family medical history concerning health, illness, mental illness, and drug and alcohol use is gathered. Other providers involved in the family's or child's care should be noted in the record (Child Protective Services, developmental programs, etc.) The medical provider should discuss the child's current status with the family, gathering information about sleeping, eating, elimination and relationship to mother or primary caregiver.

The principle of "anticipatory guidance" is useful with drug- and alcohol-involved families. Help the family anticipate what issues are likely to arise before the next well-baby visit and educate them about appropriate responses.

Subsequent visits. History concerning the child's health and development since the previous visit is always gathered. Illnesses or complications, milestones achieved, current behaviors and relationships with other family members should be noted. Ongoing anticipatory guidance is offered to the family, along with continued reinforcement of the importance of well-baby checks.

Every visit. The medical provider should observe caregiver-child interactions carefully. Is the caregiver attentive and responsive to the child's needs? Does the caregiver hold and touch child comfortably? Does the child seem comfortable with the caregiver?

The physical examination of the child should measure growth, note general physical appearance and signs, and assess development (gross and fine motor skills, language, social interaction). Laboratory tests will be scheduled as necessary, depending on the child's medical condition.

The Developmental Assessment

When a child shows signs of developmental delay, formal developmental assessment will be recommended by the medical care provider. In most cases, the assessment will provide useful information about the child's current capabilities and delays.

In many instances, the testing will be able to suggest specific steps caregivers and providers can take to help the child. And, in some cases, a series of developmental assessments over time will be able to predict a child's ultimate potential and help the family develop realistic expectations concerning a child's future abilities.

An experienced developmental specialist should complete the formal testing. Most frequently this will be a developmental or pediatric psychologist. Children who have severe delays or show significant signs of prenatal drug or alcohol exposure may need to be evaluated more intensely or more often than children with questionable or mild delays. As with other matters, each child will need individual consideration.

For most children with chemical exposures, the recommended schedule for developmental assessment is at six months, twelve months, eighteen months, then yearly between ages two and five. (For a description of commonly used assessment instruments, see Appendix C.)

Out-of-Home Placement

Proper placement for newborns with chemical exposure is an area of some controversy. Standards vary between different local governments and states. In some counties or states, a positive drug test for a newborn or its mother is enough to require out-of-home placement and the involvement of Child Protective Services (CPS).

In others areas, there must be specific indications of imminent danger to the child in addition to evidence of maternal substance use. Providers should be familiar with local and state guidelines for evaluating and reporting possible cases of abuse or neglect to Child Protective Services.

The child's welfare must be the primary consideration of all providers. For many children exposed to drugs and alcohol, one of the most powerful interventions possible is the successful integration of the child into the family unit. In the family, the child may be able to develop an essential sense of personal identity and belonging that is more difficult to attain in a series of group or foster homes. Where possible and appropriate, placement in the biological family (including the extended family) is the first choice.

In some cases, however, this is simply not possible. The mother may be continuing to use and be incapable of caring properly for the child. Newborns are fragile beings, easily injured by improper handling and easily endangered by inconsistent feeding. When an addicted or alcoholic mother is unable to provide the intensive care an infant needs, the child should be removed from her custody.

In some families, a grandmother or grandfather, aunt or the baby's father may be able to manage care of the child. This can be an excellent option for the baby. The child is still part of his or her "own" family, and may still be able to establish a relationship with the biological mother. In general, where extended family members have obtained custody of children with drug or alcohol exposure, they have been very devoted and successful in their care.

If the mother cannot care for the baby and there is no other family member who can provide care, foster care placement will be necessary. There are a number of potential problems with foster care.

Many children will be moved through multiple placements in a short period of time. This may be especially likely for children with substance exposure who require special care or intensive attention. Bonding in the foster home is sometimes less powerful for a newborn. The foster mother may be dealing with several foster children, all of whom have individual needs. Additionally, it may be difficult for a foster mother to bond fully with a child when she is uncertain how long she will have the child in her care.

The most serious problem in the foster care system is a shortage of adequate placements. There are simply not enough good foster homes to go around. Demands for foster care are increasing as the number of available homes decreases.

Cultural issues also become important in the foster care system. The majority of children in the foster care system are urban children of color, and most children with chemical exposure considered for foster care are African American or Latino. (This appears to be primarily the consequence of class privilege— middle class women with drug-affected newborns tend to have more options for care, are less likely to have been identified as maternal drug users, and are less likely to have been investigated by CPS.) There are not enough African American and Latino foster homes to care for all of the children identified as needing foster care.

Research efforts yield different opinions on the question of foster children raised in homes by parents of racial backgrounds different from their own.

Professional organizations such as the Association of Black Social Workers have publicly stated that children should be placed with a foster family of the same race. They feel strongly that the children's self-esteem and future emotional adjustment depend on their ability to bond with someone like themselves.

These views have been written into the regulations of social service departments in many states. States may attempt to provide a racial match before releasing a child to a family of a different race.

Some mothers who cannot care for their newborn children want to begin the process of recovery. Regaining custody of a child may be a strong motivating factor in the effort to stop using substances. Recovery and parent education may help a mother become capable of care at a later point in time, and providers should assist in such efforts if possible. Reunification of families is always a goal whenever it is consistent with the care and well-being of the child

Signs of Neglect and Abuse

Providers working with children from drug- and alcohol-involved families should always stay alert to warning signs of possible child neglect or abuse. These include:

- multiple missed appointments
- a parent coming to appointments high or intoxicated
- lack of physical contact between parent and child and slow parental response to the child's needs
- history of continued drug use or family violence
- poor hygiene in the child
- injuries or multiple bruises
- "failure to thrive"— inadequate weight gain or growth

A combination of the above factors, or the presence of serious injury in the child, should immediately alert providers to the potential danger for the child.

Such concerns should be discussed directly with the caregiver if possible, as well as with other agency or program staff. A report to Child Protective

Services must always be made if there is reasonable evidence to support the suspicion of neglect or abuse.

Day-to-Day Care

One of the most challenging aspects of care for children with drug and alcohol exposure is the completion of tasks related to day-to-day living. When newborns are withdrawing from drugs or alcohol, their care can be difficult. They may be fussy or irritable babies, or they may have feeding difficulties or trouble sleeping. Actions as basic as picking the child up, holding the child, feeding and diapering, can present considerable challenges to parents and other caregivers.

For premature babies and children born after crack cocaine exposure, there may be additional complications stemming from neurologic difficulties. These children have often come into the world before their neurologic systems were adequately developed. If so, they may require special kinds of attention. Caregivers may need to exercise the child in ways that stimulate continued neurologic development through the first six to twelve months of life.

Children born with prenatal alcohol exposure, especially those with full Fetal Alcohol Syndrome (the most severe manifestation), are likely to have significant difficulties in feeding, gaining weight and growing. They tend to be hypotonic (have poor muscle tone and seem generally "floppy"). Their care is not so much a matter of dealing with a fussy or irritable baby, but of supporting the baby adequately during holding and being careful during feeding.

As in other areas of care, each baby needs to be individually evaluated. Many infants have polydrug exposure, and the effects of multiple drug exposure can be confusing and somewhat unpredictable. Each child will have his or her own innate preferences as well. The recommendations below are general in nature, and what works for one child may not work for another.

Often, the extreme fussiness or feeding difficulties newborns and infants exhibit resolve within the first year of life. The most severe problems may clear up once the baby has completed drug withdrawal—anywhere from several days to two or three weeks.

The following suggestions can make these daily tasks more successful.

Picking up the baby. The basic guideline in caring for infants with drug exposure is, Take your time and don't rush. It is important in all aspects of care to avoid quick moves or actions that will startle the baby.

Infants with drug or alcohol exposure are likely to be stiff and tense. You want to provide them a sense of security when picking them up. Keeping the baby tightly swaddled will help. You can also warn the baby that you are going to be picking her up and give her time to prepare for this. Start by speaking softly to her. Then touch her gently. Massage her feet or back gently for a moment or two. At each stage, she may startle a bit. Wait until she is calmer before moving to the next step. When she is comfortable with your presence, reach down and pick her up.

Provide full support for the baby, including head support. Hold her close and keep her arms in close to your body.

This process may not become easy for several weeks with especially fussy babies. By following the same routine each time (speak softly, touch gently, massage gently, pick the baby up), you can help the baby become acclimated to the process.

For "floppy" babies, the process will not be so time consuming and not all stages will be necessary. These infants need very careful attention to head support. Be sure to provide total support for the head throughout the newborn period and beyond, until the baby repeatedly shows an ability to hold her head up by herself.

Swaddling. Most newborns, but especially those with drug or alcohol exposure, like being wrapped tightly in a soft, snug blanket. This gives them a sense of close security and control.

Lay the baby on the blanket. Keeping his hands and feet inside the blanket, wrap first one side, and then the other, tightly around him. He may struggle and push against the blanket, especially if he is a stiff and tense baby. Use common sense on how tightly to wrap the baby, and have a doctor or a nurse demonstrate this if you are not sure about how tight the blanket can be.

Holding the baby. After you have swaddled the baby and picked her up, you will want to find a comfortable position for holding her. Babies with drug exposure often are not comfortable being held the way other babies are. They may not like being gently bounced, swung or rocked while being held. They may not like "perching" up on your shoulder or being held cradle-like in your arms. They may be uncomfortable with loud speech, singing or talking. You will have to find out from each baby what she likes and dislikes.

Generally, babies with substance exposure like being held fairly tightly. They do not like to be swung up in the air with their feet or arms dangling free. Keep them tightly swaddled and hold them close to your body.

Every baby-care book encourages caregivers to look directly at their babies' faces when holding and playing with them. For babies with substance exposure, this may be too much stimulation. If a baby screams, cries or becomes agitated when placed face-to-face with a caregiver, hold her on your lap, pulled close to your body, facing away from you. You might take a simple object or toy—a colored ball or a plain colored block, for example—and move it slowly in front of the baby's eyes on occasion. The baby may not be able to follow the object with her eyes to start, but in time this often becomes possible.

After a few days, turn the baby a little bit towards you as you hold her. The next time you hold her, keep her in this new position. A little at a time, you want to turn her around until she is facing you directly. This entire process might take as long as two or three weeks. Continue to allow her to practice following the toy a few times a day during this time.

Be patient in this process. It is essential that the baby be able to look directly at her caregiver(s), but for some infants it is not possible at the time of birth. If the baby doesn't develop this ability, she may have significant emotional problems as she matures.

Some infants like being held in "Snuggli" type holders, where the child is tightly wrapped and carried in a sling in front of the caregiver. The face is turned close to the adult's body so the baby does not have the overstimulation of face-to-face contact. The body warmth and sound of the caregiver's heartbeat may also help the baby feel more secure.

Calming and soothing a crying baby. Drug exposed infants tend to cry more than other babies, and their cries may be especially painful to listen to. This can be exhausting for baby and caregiver alike.

The first task, as with any crying baby, is to understand what the baby is crying about. Is he hungry? tired? wet? Is he suffering physical pains related to birth injury or drug withdrawal? Some birth mothers feel guilty if their baby is suffering withdrawal pains—they have experienced these pains themselves and know how horrible they are. If the birth mother is involved in the child's care, it is essential that she understand her attention and care provide some of the best help for the baby's pain.

If a baby might be hungry, you can try to feed him. If he has just fed, however, it is best to wait. Too much feeding overstimulates a baby with substance exposure, and he will be likely to throw up the new food as well as the meal just completed. Some babies are able to take mild herbal teas or warm water in a bottle without throwing up, and this may calm a baby down.

Often, babies with drug or alcohol exposure are soothed by sucking, even when they are not feeding. It is fine for these babies to suck on a pacifier or on their fingers—the benefit they get from calming themselves down this way far outweighs any potential problems.

Some (but not all) babies with substance exposure enjoy the repetitive, mild stimulation of "wind-up" chairs that swing them gently. This may help a baby stop crying.

A gentle foot or ankle massage can help some stiff, tense babies relax. Their muscles and tendons get very tired from being held so rigidly, but they are unable to relax them on their own. Soft, gentle strokes on the baby's back may help him calm down and stop crying.

Warm baths help some babies calm down. So does soft talking, singing or gentle music played quietly.

In some cases, there is virtually nothing a caregiver can do to stop a baby's crying. Infants with prenatal chemical exposure often experience many discomforts that we cannot relieve. These periods can be extremely difficult for caregivers. After trying a variety of things, a caregiver may just need to let a baby cry for twenty minutes or so, before trying again. After a long period of steady crying, the caregiver should have a friend, family member, public health nurse or other helper come over and give him or her a break.

Some babies withdrawing from methadone or heroin will need prescribed medications to help them calm down. Medication of drug exposed newborns should generally be avoided, however. Only a pediatrician experienced in managing newborn withdrawal should consider prescribing medications. Over-the-counter medicines should also be avoided, unless recommended by a pediatrician experienced in managing neonatal addiction.

Changing diapers. Babies need to have their diapers changed many times a day, but the movement and motion of diaper changing can be very unpleasant for babies with substance exposure.

You may be able to get by with fewer diaper changes for some babies. This will not be possible if you have a baby who develops diaper rash easily or who is easily disturbed by wet or soiled diapers.

Ideally, you want to try to calm a baby down before beginning a diaper change. If you can help a baby stop crying and relax, the process will be easier. Sometimes, a wet or soiled diaper makes the baby so uncomfortable this is not possible.

Babies are most likely to urinate and defecate immediately after feeding. A good time to change diapers is in the sleepy state right after feeding. In general, diapers using tape will be much easier with these babies than diapers using pins.

Diaper changing should take place in slow, careful stages, one small step at a time. It may take several minutes to successfully change a diaper, even for someone who is very experienced and used to changing diapers in a moment or two.

You can start by speaking softly to the baby, touching her gently, then massaging her ankle or foot for a moment. This tells the baby she is about to be moved and handled.

Take up the tape on one side and loosen that side of the diaper. Then wait a moment or two, to let the baby calm down. Next, take up the other side of tape, and loosen that side of the diaper. Wait a moment again. Pull the diaper off the baby. If she is agitated, wait a moment before cleaning her. Clean her gently, then reverse these steps, continuing to move slowly and calmly.

There will be some "accidents" when diapers are changed this way. If a baby is fussy and stiffens during cleaning, things can get pretty messy! The baby may urinate or defecate while you are waiting for her to calm down so you can put on her clean diaper. It is important to expect this and not become upset when it happens.

Feeding. Babies born after prenatal exposure to cocaine, heroin and methadone are likely to have an uncoordinated suck and swallow reflex— they may be able to suck well, but cannot manage to swallow. Newborns with Fetal Alcohol Syndrome may have difficulty sucking and swallowing. All of these babies are likely to be small for their gestational age and have trouble keeping food down and gaining weight. Monitoring weight gain is important throughout the newborn period.

Because feeding these infants can be so difficult, it is important to be as relaxed as possible during feeding, and to have plenty of time to complete the job. Put as much effort into making *yourself* comfortable as you do into comforting the baby. Use a comfortable chair, have the room at a nice temperature (not too hot or cold), have a glass of water nearby, play some quiet music you enjoy. It may take some babies an hour or more to feed well.

If a baby grabs at a nipple and sucks vigorously until he chokes, you may need to control the amount of milk or formula the baby takes in. Let him suck a little bit, then pull the nipple out of his mouth to give him a chance to swallow and burp.

The baby may do better with many short meals over the course of the day, instead of several longer meals.

Babies with drug or alcohol exposure usually cannot be fed by "propping up" a bottle. They need a caregiver to hold the bottle for them throughout the feeding, helping to control the flow of formula and holding the bottle at the correct angle.

Some caregivers report babies exposed to crack cocaine have developed allergies or other intolerances for a particular formula. They may have asthmatic reactions. It is not clear whether prenatal cocaine exposure makes infants more sensitive to some formulas, or asthma is a complication of prenatal cocaine exposure, or some other environmental problem (dust, pets, cigarette smoke) might be involved. If a baby has trouble with one formula, however, it may be a good idea to ask your pediatrician to suggest a different one.

As the babies get older, they may have trouble with soft solid food as well. Around four to six months, a baby's diet typically expands to include cereals or pureed fruits and vegetables. Because some of the babies have a "tongue thrusting" reflex, you may put food in the baby's mouth and have him spit it right back out again.

Use a small spoon for soft solid foods. Put a small amount of food on the spoon, and put it on the middle of the baby's tongue. If the food is too far back in the mouth, the baby may gag. If it is too far forward, the baby will push the food out with his tongue.

Avoid feeding the baby formula or milk before solid foods. He may fill up on the formula and have little interest in the rest of his meal. Try giving him formula at one meal and solid food at the next.

Babies with drug and alcohol exposure may spit up solid foods more than other infants. You can try thickening liquid formula with a little rice cereal to help the baby get more accustomed to these slightly heavier foods. Avoid jiggling or bouncing the baby during feedings, and burp him frequently. You may want to put the baby in an infant seat after feeding so he is sitting upright. This can help the food stay down.

At nine to fifteen months, when the child is being weaned off soft foods and moved into toddler foods, small frequent meals will probably be most successful. He may want to help feed himself at this age. Because of the muscle and joint stiffness many babies with substance exposure continue to experience at this age, self-feeding may be difficult. Provide foods a baby with stiff hands can pick up easily—mashed fruits or vegetables, for example. Expect feeding at this stage to be very messy. Encourage the child to develop independent feeding skills, and try to make meal times pleasant and enjoyable.

Putting the baby to sleep. Infants with prenatal drug exposure often have what are called "state control problems." This means they are not able, like other children, to wake up gradually, stay awake for awhile, get sleepy and then go back to sleep. They often move from one state to another quickly, without transition, for example, going from a deep sleep to intense crying and screaming in an instant. It is hard to establish a regular sleep routine with these babies.

Caregivers should try to maintain a routine, however, even if it is not always successful. Most babies will feel a little drowsy after feeding, so try to feed the baby just before her bedtime. As she calms down, change her diapers and put her into her crib, away from loud noise or activity.

The baby can be placed on her side or back (Dwyer, 1991). It is normal for babies with substance exposure to cry before they sleep. You can try to calm the baby down, rub her back or massage her ankles, or speak softly to her. You might want to leave a couple of soft nightlights on in the room. The babies may find this reassuring even at a very early age.

Older infants. By age six to nine months, the child should have a regular evening bedtime. You can help the baby "wind down" in the hour before bed, avoiding high levels of activity, noise or distraction. Some babies will sleep better after feeding and/or bathing. Maintain a nighttime routine and try not to change it (for example, feed the baby, bathe her, give her clean diapers and pajamas, put her in her crib, play soft music, leave on a nightlight). If the baby has a favorite toy or blanket, put that in her crib, too. Sometimes "white noise," a metronome or a loudly ticking clock helps calm a baby. Don't worry if she cries a little bit while she tries to settle down.

Some children are not able to go right to sleep. They may wake up several times, crying. It is fine to go in and reassure the baby. Use the calming techniques described earlier. Do not feed the baby at night. Try to keep the baby in her own crib or bed. Do not move her to a parent's or sibling's bed when she is restless.

Sleep is generally a major problem for children with drug exposure. Expect them to be more restless than their non-exposed peers, to wake more often, to cry more, to be frightened more. Caregivers can help most by providing consistent, caring support for children during this difficult period, and maintaining patience with themselves as well as their children.

Exercise, stimulation and play. Newborns, exposed to drugs or alcohol especially those with compromised neurologic development, need help getting used to the feeling of human touch. The ability to touch and be touched by others is essential to healthy development, but they will need much more help in achieving this than non-exposed children.

The children should be touched frequently, for short periods of time, throughout the day. The touch can be very gentle, such as placing your hand on the baby's back for a moment. It can also be more active—moving the baby's legs back and forth to help work out some of the muscle and joint stiffness, for example. Caregivers can give the baby gentle massage, working on ankles, wrists and hands which tend to be especially tight.

During bathing, the child may find it easier to be washed with a soft washcloth than with another person's hand. Give him the time he needs to get used to the special feeling of human touch and avoid touch that seems very uncomfortable to him.

Keep the baby's environment from being very stimulating. For example, if you have a mobile over the baby's crib that winds up, moves around and plays music, you may want to avoid winding it up for a while. Just having an object that hangs over the crib may be adequate stimulation.

As the baby grows and begins to move about more, be careful not to push him to do things before he is ready. He may not be ready to crawl, sit or stand at this age because his muscle tone is not developed enough or he is too stiff. Expect some of the babies to attain milestones later than non-exposed children.

The baby may need more attention as he moves more independently. Because of his stiffness and neurological problems, he may be awkward or clumsy. Some children with substance exposure fall more than other babies, cannot coordinate their movements (crawling backwards instead of forwards, for example), or cannot process information quickly enough as they begin to move about and run into walls or furniture. They may not be able to break a fall with the same reflexive action non-exposed babies would use. You may need to provide extra padding (a folded blanket or cushion on the floor), or set up barriers to keep the baby from more dangerous areas (sharp table edges, ironing boards, etc.)

Sometimes the awkward movements of the infant or toddler may strike us as funny. It is important not to laugh at the child during these difficult times. The child finds his clumsiness frightening. His brain is telling him he *should* be able to move towards the brightly colored toy, and his body is unable to do so. Repeated bumps and falls can be physically painful. If the child is not protected and encouraged, he may become afraid to try to do new things. Even more than with other children, respect and encouragement is essential for these children as they develop new skills and capabilities.

Babies with substance exposure should also be spoken to frequently. This gives them an opportunity to hear words and, later, to practice words on their own. Caregivers can talk to them throughout the day. As they become more acclimated to human touch and speech, they will enjoy this kind of attention and interaction.

Quiet babies, especially babies exposed to alcohol, may be overlooked in exercise planning because they are usually compliant and their problems are less evident. These children will also benefit from talking, exercise and stimulation.

For some children with hypertonicity (muscle stiffness), physical therapy may be necessary. Those with speech delay may need hearing evaluation and speech therapy.

Remember that each child is unique, and what works for "some" or even "most" drug-affected children will not work for all. The most important skill for a caregiver or provider is the ability to read a child's signals correctly. Once these signals are clear and known, the caregiver can avoid giving a child more stimulation than he or she can handle, while observing carefully and responding appropriately when the child is ready for more.

❧ ❧ ❧

Antonio
An Infant Needing Considerable Attention

Antonio's mother Yolanda was twenty years old. She had used alcohol and crack cocaine heavily throughout her pregnancy. Antonio was her first child, and he was born full term at forty weeks gestation. His urine toxicology screen was positive for cocaine at birth.

From the outset, Antonio had many problems. He was unable to relax and continued to respond to stimuli long after most babies would have quieted or calmed down. If someone tapped the side of his crib gently, he would shake his arms and legs and grimace for several minutes. He had an excellent suck reflex—in fact, he soon developed marks on his hands and wrists from sucking on them. But he was unable to swallow food, and even the most experienced nurses had trouble getting him to take formula without choking or spitting up. Antonio often cried for hours at a time.

Antonio's mother visited him for about an hour a day. She could not feed him, did not enjoy holding him, and seemed at a loss in his company. She complained to the nurses about his crying and usually seemed as edgy and jittery as her baby.

At seven days of age, Antonio became less jittery, and feeding became easier. Yolanda's mother, Mrs. Ramirez, had begun visiting regularly and was able to feed him small amounts of formula successfully. The child was discharged in the care of his mother and grandmother. Child Protective Services, involved at the time of his birth, monitored his progress in the home. A public health nurse from the hospital also visited the home daily for two weeks, checking his feeding progress and weight gain carefully.

Follow-up: Antonio was seen at the outpatient clinic at ten days of age to maintain close scrutiny of his feeding and weight gain, as well as to check on the family's general ability to care for him. He was swallowing and feeding more easily. His muscle tone was still stiff, and he was a difficult child to hold. As his grandmother pulled him close, he would grimace, stiffen and push away from her, emitting a high-pitched piercing cry right next to her ear. "Oh, this baby can scream!" she exclaimed.

Mother and grandmother were taught to wrap Antonio tightly in a blanket. The tightness gave him a sense of security he did not have with loosely-wrapped clothing. They were also encouraged to hold him in a manner that was less stimulating and uncomfortable for him. To start with, he would be held tightly on their laps, facing forward, so he did not have to look directly into their eyes. Every few days, they were to rotate him just slightly, so that over a period of two or three weeks, he would be looking more directly at them.

Yolanda had enrolled in a drug treatment program as mandated by Child Protective Services.

One month: Antonio was seen again in the outpatient clinic at age one month, brought in by his grandmother. His mother had dropped out of the drug treatment program and was using crack heavily again. She came by the house once or twice a week to shower, eat and sleep, but was no longer living there.

Antonio's weight gain was satisfactory. His grandmother usually spent about ninety minutes on feedings. The boy was still difficult to touch, with high startle reflexes and irritability. Mrs. Ramirez was having an especially difficult time with diapering. Sometimes when she was halfway through changing a diaper she simply had to stop because Antonio had become so agitated. He would stiffen his body so that she could not move his legs, and he screamed throughout the process. The clinic staff explained to Mrs. Ramirez how to change the baby's diaper in slow-motion stages, one small step at a time.

The physician discussed Yolanda's abandonment of Antonio with Mrs. Ramirez, and his grandmother agreed that a report to Child Protective Services was in order. The report was made by the treating physician. Mrs. Ramirez was given a referral to a local support group of grandparents caring for grandchildren. Many of these families were raising children with problems similar to Antonio's and, like Mrs. Ramirez, were also coping with the special demands of caring for difficult children in their senior years.

Two months: At two months, Antonio returned with his grandmother for a well-baby visit. Mrs. Ramirez was having more success feeding him and he had gradually become more accustomed to having his diaper changed. His weight gain continued to be satisfactory. Antonio was still an agitated baby, however, who cried often and slept poorly. Sometimes he cried all night long. He did not look back at his grandmother when she held him—he seemed to look through her, not actually seeing her.

The staff shared some ideas with Mrs. Ramirez that might help calm Antonio. They suggested she try playing soft music at bedtime. She was also advised to keep a small light on in the room and to keep him on a regular routine of sleeping, napping, feeding and awakening. Mrs. Ramirez had been swaddling the baby tightly during the day, but loosening his clothing at night so he would be more comfortable. Staff suggested she try keeping him tightly wrapped at night as well.

Monthly well-baby visits were planned for the next few months to continue monitoring Antonio's progress and weight gain. The staff explained to Mrs. Ramirez that her grandson was different from other babies she had cared for. He would find it more difficult to attain his milestones. If he was like many other babies with cocaine exposure they had worked with, he might try to roll over at the appropriate time (about six months), but his body would be too rigid for him to succeed. He would probably want to hold his own bottle at age six to eight months, but be unable to loosen his hands so they could wrap around the bottle comfortably.

Three months: At the next visit, Antonio's progress was again satisfactory. Yolanda continued to drop by the house on occasion, but showed only minimal interest in Antonio. Mrs. Ramirez had given her money a number of times to "buy some clothes so she could look for a job." Each time, however, Yolanda disappeared again.

Antonio's feeding had improved considerably by this time, and Mrs. Ramirez was often able to complete a feeding in 45 minutes. He had become accustomed to diaper changes and seemed to enjoy soft music at bedtime. On a few occasions, he had looked directly at Mrs. Ramirez. His grandmother's sense of being "seen" by Antonio added immensely to the gratification she gained from caring for this difficult baby. He was noted at this visit to track visually, though in a limited range, and to respond intermittently to auditory stimuli.

A drug counselor was able to speak with Mrs. Ramirez at this visit. She told him about her daughter Yolanda, "who is breaking my heart." She asked him how she could help Yolanda stop using drugs and become a good mother to Antonio.

The counselor offered to see Mrs. Ramirez on a regular basis. Over the course of several weeks, he explained to her the typical behavior of chemically dependent people. Mrs. Ramirez also began to understand ways she had enabled Yolanda to use drugs—helping her by providing money, excusing behaviors, getting her out of trouble, and so forth. She began to attend a local support group for families and friends of addicts and alcoholics, and through the group learned that she could not expect to change Yolanda's behavior. This was something Yolanda would have to do for herself. Mrs. Ramirez used the support group to help her cope with her great sadness about her daughter's addiction.

Antonio's future remains unclear. At three months of age, he continued to show some signs of neurologic injury. He had been improving steadily, however, with the skillful and consistent care his grandmother had offered. The clinic staff was unable to predict for Mrs. Ramirez what Antonio's future potential would be. They were able to reassure her, however, that her excellent care was responsible in large part for the improvement he had shown thus far, and would continue to be of immeasurable value to him in the future.

Comment: *Antonio's story is typical of newborns and infants who have suffered more severe effects of prenatal cocaine exposure. He required considerable attention and patience in his newborn period. He is lucky to have a grandmother who is physically and emotionally capable of providing loving and consistent care.*

With our current limited knowledge of crack cocaine's longer-term effects, it is not possible to predict whether Antonio will have significant problems as he matures, only moderate ones, or no problems at all. Though he currently shows signs of neurologic injury, he has also begun to bond with his grandmother. He may be one of the children who is able to "catch up" over time, or he may have later difficulties in motor coordination, cognition and social relationships. The clinic will follow his development carefully and recommend special interventions as necessary (hearing and speech evaluation, physical therapy, therapeutic nursery, etc.).

❧ ❧ ❧

Chapter 8

What to Expect from School-Age Children

"I have this boy in my first grade class. I cannot do a thing with him. He has an incredibly short attention span. He is easily distracted. He is clumsy, always bumping into things and knocking them over. He writes poorly. Can't read well. Doesn't retain information. He is very impulsive, and on a few occasions has struck out at other children.

"I believe he is a 'crack kid,' and while it makes me very sad to say so, I do not have much hope that I can help him or that he will achieve much in his school life."

—Teacher

Tales like the one described above are being told all around the country. Teachers have been warned by news reports of the severe and tragic effects of prenatal crack cocaine exposure, and have been prepared for an onslaught of students who are impossible to control and have little chance of learning. The best hope in some of these stories is that special education programs will be able to handle these children.

Special education programs, meanwhile, are often already overtaxed. Teachers in these programs are as concerned as anyone else about these difficult students that will be overwhelming their classes. In some areas, there has been serious discussion of opening entire schools dedicated to the management and education of children exposed prenatally to crack cocaine.

Readers of news magazines have been educated about the kinds of problems "crack kids" will have: short attention spans, difficulty learning, impulsiveness, aggressive behavior.

The boy in the story above certainly fits that profile, so it is not surprising that his teacher assumes he has a prenatal history of crack exposure. Nor is it surprising that she feels defeated by his problems and unable to help—few have suggested so far that the situation might be otherwise!

The truth of the matter is that most teachers will not know if a student has had prenatal exposure to crack cocaine or other substances. This confidential medical information is not generally included in a student record unless parents choose to release the information, and most parents prefer not to do so. Teachers and other school personnel, as well as those who work with children in community settings, may have nothing more to go on than the child's individual behavior in the classroom or program.

While this may seem to frustrate efforts to help children with drug and alcohol exposure, a closer look at the issue will reveal the wisdom behind such policies. The label "crack kid," or "fetal alcohol effect," or "chemically exposed infant" does not tell us what we can expect from an individual child.

Though we can describe the trends seen among groups of children with a particular prenatal exposure, each child is a complex interrelationship of environment and innate ability. We cannot know, without assessing the individual child properly and carefully, what his or her particular strengths and challenges are likely to be.

The teacher in our opening story has already accomplished part of the work necessary with her student. She can describe the nature of his difficulties and give specific examples of his behavior to back up her observations. Now she needs to take the process a step further.

She must decide if the severity of his problems warrants an individual assessment of his developmental, social and learning capabilities (it does); and then develop strategies to respond to his particular areas of difficulty and enhance his areas of strength and capability. Despite her current sense of frustration, there is quite a bit she can do for the boy.

The most severely affected children with prenatal chemical exposure will be clearly identified before they reach regular school age. They will most likely be involved in special programs before kindergarten, and will continue to participate in special education programs throughout their school careers. But this will be a relatively small number overall.

The greater portion of children born with drug or alcohol exposure will be placed into mainstream school classes and will participate freely in other community-based programs. They will interact with their peers and with adults, develop increasing independence from their families, and begin to demonstrate characteristic styles of learning and responding to new information. Like other children, the newness of the school environment will challenge them, and, like other children, they will respond to the challenge in different ways.

Challenges in the School Environment

In the most general terms, we should expect that a significant portion of children with prenatal chemical exposure will have learning difficulties of some sort. The particular type of difficulty will be influenced by the specific chemicals used during the pregnancy, the point of fetal development at which they were used, the amounts used, and the mixtures of different drugs used.

For these children, the most common difficulties will be in understanding and processing information. There may also be problems with language, coordination, attention span and impulsivity. Some will have additional physical problems, including hearing impairment, visual problems, slow growth, clumsiness and problems with fine motor coordination.

The families of children with substance exposure may also be challenged by a child's attendance at school. They may be troubled and chaotic, too disorganized to become fully involved in their child's educational program. The increased independence of the school-age child may threaten the family—they may worry that the child will say things about them in the public setting of school that they would rather leave unsaid.

The child's increased vulnerability in the school setting may also frighten the family; outsiders will not understand the child the way the family does. The potential intrusiveness of school personnel can be distasteful to drug- and alcohol-involved families. Some families will feel resentful of the child's new attachments to teachers or other providers and may sabotage these relationships in subtle or not-so-subtle ways.

Children making a transition to school settings from a therapeutic nursery may also face some special challenges. They will be spending less time with people who have provided consistent and loving care for them. They must face the uncertainty of forming attachments with new teachers and classmates. The intensity of individualized attention available in the therapeutic nursery will not be available in the regular school classroom.

Their behavior may regress. They may act like younger children, and they may revert to old problem behaviors that had largely resolved. These children will need special support during the transition period, some of which may be provided by the nursery program staff.

These are not new problems for teachers or others working with children.

Anyone who has worked with young children for very long has worked with children who have poor impulse control, who have difficulty learning to read, who misbehave, who fight with other children. Anyone who has worked with family members of young children has come across chaotic and dysfunctional families. Teachers and others have helped children before who have needed support when making major transitions in their lives.

Competent professionals in child services learned long ago that such children need individual attention and individualized strategies in response to the difficulties they face. When children demonstrate problems of this nature, it is appropriate to refer them for assessment by a developmental specialist, to evaluate the need for an Individualized Educational Program (IEP), and to work with the family and school to develop a program appropriate to the particular strengths and challenges of the child.

The Full Range of Influences

It is important that children whose behavior fits the popular "profile" of a child with substance exposure not automatically be considered to have significant limitations in potential. Things that could be done for the child and his or her family may be overlooked, and wrong assumptions could be made. It is always possible that drug exposure is not even the basis of the problem.

> "I hear from teachers that they are feeling increasingly stressed by students who are poorly prepared for the school setting. Often they ask if these difficulties are not the result of the drug epidemic, of parents' use of substances during a pregnancy. Perhaps this is so in some cases.
>
> "But there are other possibilities too. These problems, in fact, may be rooted in the abject poverty and incredible violence many children today are exposed to. I worked in the South Bronx 15 years ago, and it was considered a 'tough' neighborhood then. I can tell you that the neighborhood today is so much more impoverished, the violence is so much greater, it doesn't even resemble the place I used to know. It doesn't surprise me one bit to hear that teachers in these areas are seeing unprecedented amounts of learning and behavioral

> problems among their students. But I don't think you could assume, without knowing an individual child's history, that the problems stem from prenatal drug exposure."
>
> —Public health nurse

Increasingly, students from disorganized families are entering the school system, bringing with them family histories that include parental substance abuse, family violence, parental depression or emotional disturbance, physical and sexual abuse of children, and neglect. These problems occur across socioeconomic lines but poverty, with its attendant hopelessness and lack of access to resources, can significantly worsen already difficult situations.

Children are deeply affected by their family's circumstances and events in their neighborhoods. Children who are poorly nourished, who live in a violent neighborhood, who have seen people shot and killed, who are taking medications for illnesses, who have problems with hearing or vision—any of these children may manifest the kinds of behaviors seen in the boy described in the opening quotation. It is important that we not overlook the full range of influences on children's lives when we consider whether their difficulties are related to prenatal drug or alcohol exposure. If we do, we may miss useful opportunities to intervene and help.

Medical Care

Medical care for children in early elementary grades who have experienced prenatal chemical exposure should continue to be a partnership between providers and families. Teachers should be advised of specific medical problems that may need special attention or care in the classroom setting. People working with the child in community programs should be similarly advised.

Health care follow-up for older children should follow guidelines similar to those for infants and toddlers. Visits should include a careful report of the child's current status and note important events or changes since the last visit. Observations of caregiver-child interactions continue to be important, and should be evaluated and assessed by the provider.

Developmental milestones should continue to be recorded and assessed.

Physical exams should be completed, with particular attention paid to difficulties in language, hearing and vision that may become more apparent as the child enters school.

The medical visit also continues to provide opportunities for caregiver education about the child's ongoing development. Anticipatory guidance can prepare the family for challenges they and their child may face as regular school begins. Depending on the child's developmental level, he or she may also be involved in prevention education, including the establishment of good health practices (brushing teeth, eating well) and avoiding injuries (pedestrian and car injuries, falls and drownings, gun violence).

Myths About Learning Needs

There are a number of myths about what it is like to teach or work with children born chemically exposed. We offer responses to some of the most common.*

- ***Myth:*** *"Crack kids" are the most severely affected of all children born with substance exposure. Crack is the most dangerous drug.*

  Fact: Children with prenatal crack cocaine exposure are usually suffering polydrug exposure. Mothers who used crack often have also used cigarettes, marijuana and alcohol. The severe effects seen in some children exposed to crack before birth may be the result of considerable drug combinations throughout the pregnancy.

  With appropriate, intensive interventions, many of these children have caught up more dramatically than children with other drug exposures.

  Each drug poses its own particular dangers to a developing fetus and to family function. It is misleading to say one drug is "more dangerous" than another. (See Chapter 3 for more about the special features of crack.)

- ***Myth:*** *Children with prenatal drug or alcohol exposure are irreparably damaged, and have little chance of becoming self-supporting or satisfied as adults.*

* This list of myths has been adapted and expanded from a list originally written by Sandra Jackson (1990).

Fact: We cannot say for certain how well any child will succeed in his or her adult life. We can say that many children with substance exposure are doing extremely well with appropriate intervention and education—as well as their non-exposed peers in a good number of cases. We expect the majority of these children to lead normal, healthy lives.

- ***Myth:*** *Children with prenatal drug and alcohol exposure are substantially different from children without such exposure.*

  Fact: Children exposed to drugs or alcohol are more like their peers than unlike them.

- ***Myth:*** *Most children born drug or alcohol exposed are found in poor, urban neighborhoods.*

  Fact: Children with prenatal substance exposure have most frequently been identified in poor urban neighborhoods. But substance abuse occurs along all socioeconomic, geographic and racial lines. Careful attention would identify children affected by drugs and alcohol in virtually all neighborhoods.

- ***Myth:*** *Most of these children are African American, as are the majority of mothers who use drugs and alcohol.*

  Fact: The African American community is bearing an extraordinary amount of the pain and suffering of the crack epidemic, as well as of other drug-use trends. This has more to do with the placement of the drug trade in poor Black neighborhoods and the incredible ease of access to drugs in such places. Drug and alcohol use, including crack cocaine use, crosses all socioeconomic, geographic, racial and ethnic lines.

- ***Myth:*** *Children with drug or alcohol exposure are uneducable.*

  Fact: Children learn in different ways. Children born drug or alcohol exposed are more likely than their non-exposed peers to experience problems in learning and processing new information. With proper planning, teachers and others who work with these children will find most of them capable of learning a great deal.

- ***Myth:*** *Children with drug and alcohol exposure will usually be placed in special education programs, and regular classroom teachers will not need to know how to work with them.*

Fact: Most children will be placed in regular classroom settings. They may require special attention in some areas of learning. Regular classroom teachers will work with the largest portion of children with substance exposure.

- ***Myth:*** *Children with substance exposure will be so severely disabled they will be unlikely to participate in community-based programs; staff in those programs will not need to know how to work with them.*

  Fact: Children born chemically exposed will benefit from opportunities to socialize with groups of peers. We should expect to see them in community-based programs and make adaptations for them as necessary to help them feel welcome and ensure that they succeed in their experience.

- ***Myth:*** *Teachers and others who work with children will need an extraordinary amount of training to be able to work successfully with children with drug and alcohol exposure.*

  Fact: Most teachers are already using many of the techniques useful for the special needs of the child with substance exposure. These techniques are fairly straightforward and easy to learn. Some training will be helpful, especially for providers less familiar with theories and practical applications of learning styles. Extraordinary amounts of training will not be necessary.

- ***Myth:*** *Children exposed prenatally to crack cocaine, and other children with prenatal drug exposures, will be inexorably drawn to a life of addiction themselves when they reach adolescence.*

  Fact: We do not know at present whether these children will have greater susceptibility to chemical dependency than their non-exposed peers. We do know that children from families with a chemically dependent parent are more likely to develop dependencies as adolescents and adults.

  With the state of the drug epidemic today, it is clear that *all* children need aggressive, comprehensive drug and alcohol prevention education throughout their school careers. These programs can be started as early as kindergarten and first grade and do not need to be specially tailored in any way for the child with chemical exposure.

- ***Myth:*** *These children are aggressive, uncontrollable and criminally violent.*

  Fact: Some (not all) children born chemically exposed have difficulties with impulse control and aggression. The outbursts such children display are not the result of criminal intention. They are a response to stimulation in their environment, or to an internal, possibly neurologic impulse.

  Impulsive children usually respond well to appropriate attention and limit-setting behaviors. Most who have received consistent therapeutic interventions at an early age exhibit improved control of impulses and diminished aggressiveness, and they are able to socialize properly as they mature.

Children born drug and alcohol exposed can learn, and can contribute to their school and their community. Teachers and others who work with children do not need magic to succeed with children who have substance exposure. They will, however, benefit from knowledge, experience and understanding. Trainings on learning styles and behavioral management of difficult children will be especially helpful. (For more detailed descriptions of learning styles, see Chapter 9.)

Labeling Children: Does It Help?

> "I know a lot of teachers these days are talking about identifying children with substance exposure in school. It's difficult for us because we don't have the children's medical histories and we may have to operate on our own conjecture, based on what we know about the child's family, his or her behavior in the classroom, and so on. But I think about it this way: if you don't know a child is drug exposed, you teach him the best way you can. You figure out what's going to work with that kid, and then do it. If you do know a child has a history of drug exposure—well, you just teach those kids too, the same way. So I think the main thing we have to do to prepare to deal with crack-exposed or other 'exposed' kids is just to teach them the best we can. Just like we always have."
>
> —Teacher

In a classic study in the field of social psychology, an unusual route was taken in assessing learning behaviors in students (Rosenthal and Jacobsen, 1989). Researchers assessed the IQ levels of students in several classrooms and then provided scores on each student to teachers. The IQ scores reported, however, were not the students' actual scores. The researchers found that regardless of the level of a student's actual initial score, the students who had been "given" high IQ scores improved performance over time, and those described as having low IQ's performed more poorly.

The study revealed that teacher attention, interesting student assignments, and high expectations from teachers are powerful incentives to learning. This study also demonstrated that labels can be extraordinarily penalizing if they are used in a way that is not helpful to the student.

Most educational professionals today agree that labeling children in the school system is only justified if the label is descriptive, instructive and prescriptive. That is, it must describe for parents and teachers something about how a child learns, instruct on teaching approaches likely to succeed, and prescribe specific planning strategies that are suited to the child's learning and developmental needs.

However, the question of whether to withhold or share information about a student's prenatal chemical exposure in the school setting is a controversial one. Is this helpful labeling, or does it damage a child? Many teachers are especially frustrated that they have had little training on the special learning needs their students may present.

While most acknowledge that teacher expectation is extremely important for a student's success, they also want a realistic picture of what a student can do. If knowledge about a child's prenatal history might enlighten the teacher, it would seem to be in the student's best interest to share that knowledge.

We agree that teachers need and deserve good information and training on learning styles and multimodal teaching. (See Chapter 9 for further discussion.) They should also be given clear information about the real capabilities of a student with learning or behavioral difficulties. The problem with the labels commonly used with children who have had prenatal chemical exposures is that they do not give us this kind of information.

"Drug exposed." "Crack kid." "Methadone baby." These terms do not tell us whether a child will learn best in short interactive sessions, or by working independently on longer-range projects. They do not establish realistic expectations about a child's capabilities. They do not inform us of a child's social skills or physical talents.

The fact is, children with drug or alcohol exposure span such a wide continuum of capability and deficit that simple categories are not of much use. To fit all of these children into one or two categories would be inaccurate and would penalize many of them unfairly. Our only reasonable option is to evaluate each child individually, and utilize descriptors relevant to that child's strengths and weaknesses.

The Limitations of Labeling

Consider, for a moment, that you are a third grade teacher. You have a student who seems to be capable of learning new information during class and enjoys socializing with other children. But he also disrupts the class frequently, and his homework is usually messy and late. You discover that his mother used alcohol and cocaine during her pregnancy with the boy. Does this information help you address the child's school problems?

Not really. Perhaps, because of his prenatal exposure, he has some neurologic or cognitive problems that inhibit his ability to organize his work. It may be a great accomplishment for this boy to turn in his homework at all, even if it is messy or late. In that case, your expectations would be "lowered," and it would be appropriate to praise him for his success when he brings his work in.

On the other hand, he might simply be slacking off on some of the homework because no one is helping him learn to organize his after-school time appropriately. In this instance, you would want to encourage him to work harder on his homework, and let him know you expect a better performance.

Perhaps his mother is still involved in drug and alcohol use, and the boy feels inadequate or unable to do the work. Then you might praise his competencies in the classroom, and reassure him that he is capable of doing his work well. Maybe he does not have time to do his homework because he has responsibility for younger siblings after school. You might be able to set up a special after-school study hall for him, or refer the family to a free after-school childcare program.

The teacher of this boy does need more information, just as the teacher in this chapter's opening quotation does. But the label "cocaine exposed" or "alcohol exposed" will not help. A careful assessment of the student's learning styles, emotional status and cognitive development might.

What Teachers Need

Teachers need and deserve support in their efforts to teach an increasingly challenging student population. Their work will be more effective when communities provide adequate funding for school programs; when schools can utilize comprehensive testing services for students needing learning, behavioral, cognitive or emotional assessments; when administrators arrange teacher trainings that describe the learning and social needs of at-risk children, including children who have had prenatal chemical exposures, and teach strategies for working with such children; and when teachers are given access to well-supplied professional libraries that provide further background and information.

It is not surprising that in the absence of many of these basic resources, teachers feel increasingly frustrated at the difficulties presented by their students.

The funding and resource problems faced by many schools today are an absolute tragedy. We know that budgets have gotten tighter and in many schools essential services have been cut. It is difficult for teachers to continue to seek creative solutions for their classroom challenges. Teachers are getting tired of all the extra demands being placed on them.

We also know that the extraordinary limitations of labels commonly used for children with prenatal chemical exposure have the potential to exploit all the weaknesses of a school or system. Children could easily be "tracked" by uninformed or overworked school personnel, and their learning potentials might remain undiscovered and unidentified throughout their school careers.

> "I was asked to evaluate a half dozen children in a kindergarten class because the teacher was feeling unable to manage several of her new students. This was an experienced and dedicated teacher who had been very successful in the past, but suddenly she found herself stumped by the extreme rambunctiousness of these six students.

"In the course of observing and interviewing the children and their parents, I discovered that three of the students had had prenatal drug exposure. While I think it's possible, even probable, that this contributed to their disruptiveness, I made a clinical decision that this information would not be useful to their teacher.

"Instead, I developed learning and behavioral profiles on all six students. These really were hard kids to work with, and this teacher deserved some help. I relabeled a lot of the children's behavior—instead of calling Ricky 'disruptive,' we talked about seeing him as an 'active learner.' Christopher wasn't 'hostile and aggressive' as much as he was a child who needed help feeling more in control of his environment. The relabeling was accurate, so it worked.

"We set up a lot of practical solutions: figured out ways to set limits with the kids more successfully, discovered that two of the children were easily overstimulated and needed more quiet down-time than other students, spent more time on transitions with one of the children, got a teacher's aide in for a few extra hours a week.

"After the teacher implemented these changes, the kids calmed down quite a bit, and the class proceeded more smoothly. So the problem really wasn't that she had children with drug exposure in her class—which is fortunate, because she couldn't do anything about that. But she could do something about the easily distracted, active learners. You see my point? Labeling the kids as 'drug-exposed' wouldn't have helped anybody, but finding labels that described a problem and suggested a solution helped a lot."

—Developmental psychologist

In general, labels which indicate a child has experienced prenatal drug or alcohol exposure will not be useful in the school or community setting. Labels describing learning styles ("kinesthetic learner"), behavioral attributes ("energetic and active"), or social capabilities ("shy and quiet") can be more practical because they suggest steps a teacher or other provider can take to reinforce strengths or address weaknesses.

Diagnostic labels that describe specific attention disorders ("attention deficit disorder with hyperactivity") or learning problems ("difficulties with visual organization") likewise prescribe actions that will help the child.

"Drug-exposed" is a term which refers to a medical condition. It can inform a physician of specific problems to look for and important assessments to make. It has no similar utility for the teacher or provider outside the health arena, especially those who work with school-age children. In school settings, in fact, such a label is more likely to handicap a child unfairly. We encourage educators to use the labels of their profession when working with students, and hope the label "drug-exposed" will stay where it belongs—in the confidential arena of a child's medical record.

❧ ❧ ❧

Savannah
A Kindergartner with Special Learning Needs

Savannah was a five-year-old girl who lived with her legal guardian, Ms. Jones. Ms. Jones contacted the school district and asked that an assessment of Savannah be completed before she entered kindergarten. She knew that the girl's development was delayed, and wondered whether she would be able to benefit from a regular kindergarten class.

Ms. Jones was a sales clerk at an upscale department store. When she took her breaks, she left the store through the employee exit in an alley. There she had often encountered a pregnant woman who was obviously also a heroin addict. Ms. Jones began to bring food to the woman because she was concerned about the nutritional status of the developing fetus. She frequently spoke to the woman about her pregnancy, and a time or two encouraged her to try to get treatment for her heroin addiction.

The woman was not at her usual place one day when Ms. Jones arrived at work. She did not appear over the next two days. On the third day, returning from her break, Ms. Jones found a small bundle by the store door. In the bundle was a newborn baby, along with a note from the mother. Ms. Jones attempted to locate the woman without success. She cared for the baby during this period, and was later awarded legal guardianship of Savannah.

Savannah had been followed by a pediatrician at a local health clinic, and her mildly delayed milestones had been noted. Physically she was a healthy child, somewhat small for her age. She had been fussy and irritable in her newborn period, but these early problems had resolved. Ms. Jones was extremely attached to Savannah, and the two had an affectionate, loving relationship.

The school psychologist carried out a developmental assessment on Savannah. She tested in the average range for verbal, abstract/visual and quantitative reasoning. Her short term memory skills were in the low average range. She had difficulty sequencing information and remembering information that was presented visually. If she was allowed to keep visual information in front of her for copying, drawing or bead designs, she was able to do much better.

Savannah's emotional and social adjustment seemed excellent. She was charming, interactive and obviously felt secure with her caregiver. She was not a clinically "hyperactive" child. She was able to attend patiently to the test items she found intriguing. Her activity level increased with tasks she found difficult, as well as during periods of unstructured time. Her behavior throughout the assessment was friendly and appropriate.

Based on the findings of this assessment, Ms. Jones was informed that Savannah was a child of average intellectual ability who had a learning disability in visual sequential memory skills. She would most likely have particular difficulties with tasks such as remembering the order of the alphabet if she had to write it on paper. Her friendly personality and her secure attachment to Ms. Jones would both serve her well in her social development.

To give Savannah a good head start in the academic system, the psychologist recommended she be enrolled in a highly structured regular kindergarten. With the help of school district personnel, a class of this nature was identified. Additionally, Ms. Jones was referred to a learning specialist at a local teacher's college who would be able to help Savannah strengthen her visual memory skills.

Comment: *Savannah provides us with another example of the importance of consistent, loving care. She is a child who can be expected to perform at an* *average level in regular school if she is given special attention and support for her learning disability.*

If Savannah had not had the benefit of Ms. Jones's excellent care, her emotional development might have been considerably impaired. Without her charming personality and pleasant interpersonal skills, Savannah would find it more difficult to succeed in an academic environment. If, additionally, her specific learning disability had not been identified, this child might have started out her school career with multiple failures and disappointments. Instead, her caregiver was given specific and concrete recommendations to help her succeed.

At the time of this writing, Savannah is finishing up first grade. She is learning to read, though she still has moderate difficulty with sequencing skills. Her mathematics, verbal presentations, motor skills and social skills development are considered average to above average. She is reported by teachers to be a motivated learner whose skill base is developing nicely.

❧ ❧ ❧

Robert
A Second Grader in Family Therapy

Robert was an eight-year-old boy attending second grade. He lived with his adoptive parents, the Katzes, a professional family who had taken him into their care when he was five years old. His adoption had become final at age six and a half. He was the only child in his family.

Robert's birth parents had both used illegal substances, his mother using throughout her pregnancy. The specific types of substances used by his birth mother were not known to Mr. and Mrs. Katz. The baby was voluntarily placed into foster care after his birth, where he had lived in a succession of homes before his adoption by the Katzes.

Robert's teacher had discussed his school performance with his parents. She described him as an anxious child, immature compared to his peers, who interacted poorly with the other children. He had no close friends among his classmates, and spent most of his time at recess by himself. She acknowledged that Robert was a bright boy who applied himself well in subjects he liked. He had little patience in subjects that did not interest him, and in these areas his work was poor and his attitude unconcerned.

Recently, she felt that Robert was becoming more impulsive in his behaviors, showing poor control on a number of occasions. He misbehaved in class, but his transgressions were usual solitary in nature—walking around the class when he was supposed to be in his seat, sneaking in a soft drink after lunch and spilling it all over the floor, drawing on his desk with indelible markers. He had been disciplined on several occasions for picking on younger children at the school. The teacher called the Katzes in after an incident where Robert had singled out the smallest first grader on campus, jumped on him, and pushed his face into the dirt.

Mr. and Mrs. Katz shared the teacher's concern. Some of Robert's behaviors at home were similar, especially that he did not play with children in the neighborhood. He was occasionally belligerent with his parents, and on a few recent occasions had misbehaved in a particularly provocative way. When Mr. Katz chastised Robert for neglecting to take out the trash, the boy very deliberately went into the kitchen and dumped the trash all over the floor, then walked out of the house and was not seen again for several hours. His parents cared about him, but felt uncertain that Robert loved them or was happy in his home. They found it difficult to be physically affectionate with him—since he had arrived in their home, he had drawn away from hugs or kisses and seemed to dislike being touched.

Robert's parents, on his teacher's advice, brought him to the Developmental Pediatrics practice at a nearby university hospital. The team of providers involved in his assessment included a pediatrician, a speech and language specialist, a learning specialist and a psychologist.

On physical examination, the pediatrician found Robert to be a healthy boy. His hearing and vision were normal, his muscle tone was good and his neurologic signs were normal. He acted somewhat immaturely during his exam, talking in a babyish voice and starting to cry when a stethoscope was placed on his chest.

The speech and language specialist found no deficiencies in speech or language. The learning specialist found him to be a very bright boy, without specific learning disabilities, who was able to do work above his grade level.

The psychologist provided a developmental assessment of Robert. His results placed him in the superior range of cognitive ability. His verbal abilities were weaker than his performance abilities.

Robert's difficulties became more evident during the psychologist's exploration of his emotional development. It appeared that as a result of his numerous foster placements, Robert had never formed a strong emotional attachment to another person. He was feeling increasingly anxious because he expected at any time to be removed from his parents' care and placed again with strangers. In play therapy sessions, Robert repeatedly acted out themes of abandonment.

In a number of instances, for example, baby animals were lost or given away by their families. In one elaborate play sequence, a "space boy" had lost contact with his extraterrestrial parents and would not be able to locate them again until he had found a magic potion. Despite intense and active searching throughout the play room, the space boy was not able to find his potion or his parents.

The assessment team found Robert's cognitive, academic and speech skills to be well above average for his age. His areas of difficulty seemed to stem from an early history of unstable and unreliable attachments. Consequently, they recommended family therapy for Robert and his parents, focusing on the facilitation of deeper emotional attachments among them. Additionally, the team developed a behavior modification plan to help his teacher and his parents improve Robert's participation in school work and home chores.

Outcome: Robert, his family and his school learned new approaches for managing his troublesome behaviors, based primarily on "logical consequences" for misbehavior and intermittent positive reinforcement for more adaptive behaviors. Robert resisted changes in his behavior early in this program—his misbehavior, in fact, seemed to increase for a period of time. His teacher and parents maintained weekly contact through the first month of the program, however, and continued to provide consistent feedback to the boy. After his initial period of rebellion, Robert's behavior improved considerably.

At the same time, family therapy sessions offered repeated opportunities for Robert to express his apprehensions to his parents, and for his parents to reassure him of their love and commitment. As therapy proceeded, Mr. and Mrs. Katz found it easier to demonstrate their caring for Robert, touching him affectionately when they were together. Robert's father made it a regular practice to talk alone with Robert for a few minutes every night before the boy went to sleep. His mother planned special outings with him once a week and, on one occasion, Robert asked if he could invite the neighbor's child, Henry, who was six, to come along.

In school, Robert continued to be a loner at many recess sessions, but his teacher noticed he was somewhat more involved in team activities during physical education. She saw him reach out to a classmate during one recess session, but Robert was rebuffed by this very popular boy. Because Robert was an excellent reader, she arranged to have him spend time once a week helping out a first grader who was having reading problems. She could not say that Robert had blossomed, exactly, but he seemed to be a stronger and slightly happier child.

Comment: *Robert's early upbringing had been a difficult one. His school problems seemed to point to many of the possible effects of prenatal substance exposure, and he was known to have such a history. Fortunately, a careful evaluation of Robert's strengths and areas of difficulty clarified that his problems stemmed primarily from the emotional injuries he suffered through his early childhood years—injuries that arose because he was born into a drug-involved family. With continued care and concern from teachers and parents, this boy can be expected to make continued improvements in school performance and personal relationships.*

❧ ❧ ❧

Chapter 9

Learning Styles and Teaching Strategies

All children are learners, and they learn in a variety of ways all the time. Everything they see, hear, touch and smell provides them with worlds of information which they then incorporate into their lives in their own unique fashion.

We can gain some ready information about children's learning styles by reflecting on our own ways of learning. If you think of some of the learning tasks during your life that you have found easy, and then recall others that have been more difficult, you will be able to describe your own learning styles.

You might find that you learn best when you can see or hear things. You might learn best by reading. Or you might be the kind of person who needs to touch and experience something, to walk through it one time, to really understand it well.

Providers who teach children tend to bring their own individual learning styles to that work. We teach children in ways that were successful for us. But when we work with a variety of children, it is important to remember that our favored method of learning is only one of a number of styles.

We live in a culture that tends to measure intelligence primarily by a person's ability to speak and process information. The most highly valued intelligence is a sort of "chess player logic" found in people who are very analytic, and who can communicate their analyses through verbal means. This is a wonderful intelligence to have, but it certainly is not the only kind. If we overlook children who exhibit their intelligence in other ways, we miss opportunities to help them succeed in life and contribute meaningfully to their communities.

> "I recently read a column where the writer had been appalled while having a conversation with a well-known and highly respected filmmaker. In person, this filmmaker completely lacked the eloquence of his films. But the columnist missed the point! The filmmaker's skills were uneven. He was exceptionally talented in his ability to communicate visually, to think things through and then present his ideas on the screen. He was a visual learner. His verbal communication skills were weaker.
>
> "What better career for this obviously intelligent man than

> filmmaking, where the visual image provides the most powerful part of the experience!"
>
> —Learning specialist

A quick assessment of people's career choices and hobbies can instruct us about the ways they learn. A photographer is most likely a visual learner. A dancer is a kinesthetic learner tuned in to the way things feel and are organized in space. An engineer may have excellent visual analysis skills. Children's preferences in play and school can also give us information about how they are able to learn if we observe them carefully.

> "I want to tell you the story of my friend, Joseph. When he was a child, people thought he was unintelligent because he didn't use standard English. Teachers said he was 'slow' because he couldn't 'communicate.' He was put in Special Education, wasn't given challenging school work, and wasn't expected to succeed at anything of importance. Joseph was angry through all of this because he knew he wasn't stupid.
>
> "As an adult, Joseph went on to build an educational software business that has been extremely successful. His company specializes in designing teaching materials for students whose learning needs have not always been successfully met in the traditional school system. His materials are used by school districts around the country, and are being made available to men and women in the armed services.
>
> "How was a 'slow' student in Special Education classes able to achieve so much when he seemed capable in school of learning so little? Joseph had remarkable dedication, but he also had good luck. When he was a community college student, an instructor recognized Joseph's commitment to learning despite his academic weaknesses. He offered Joseph special attention, helped him develop an understanding of his own style of learning, and believed in his intelligence and his capabilities."
>
> —School psychologist

There are tens of thousands of "Josephs" in our schools. These students are ready and willing to learn if we present information to them in ways they can understand. They may look like they are not paying attention—always in and out of their seats, asking questions at all the wrong times. We might be tempted to call them hyperactive or behaviorally disordered, but many of these children are simply kinesthetic learners. They learn by doing.

Kinesthetic learners are often treated as behavioral problems; we put the child in a seat and say, "Don't speak unless you're called upon." We do not provide learning tasks that allow the child to use his or her well-developed sense of touch and high level of energy. We are telling the child, essentially, "You are not teachable because you won't learn my way."

It is not news that children learn in different ways. But the culture of education, which has traditionally valued linear and analytic approaches to understanding learning, continues to provide teachers today with limited instructional strategies. Teachers have often been ill-prepared to work with the complex challenges presented by the varied children in their large classrooms. Teachers can teach children with many different learning styles, and teach them well, given the proper training and support for doing so.

Learning Styles and Children with Substance Exposure

Children with prenatal chemical exposure are more likely than their non-affected peers to have learning difficulties and to need a variety of teaching techniques to successfully grasp the important concepts of their education. They may be less likely to learn in the linear, analytic style often emphasized in school systems.

The techniques and strategies we describe in the remainder of this chapter have not been developed especially for children with drug and alcohol exposure. These are methods that are applicable to all students and the variety of learning needs they will present in a classroom.

The techniques will cost little. They require only a bit of time, some flexibility, and a willingness on the part of teachers to challenge common perceptions about how children learn. All children will benefit from these techniques, but they will be of particular benefit for children at risk for school failure. If we know how a child learns, and if we teach that child in the way he or she can best process information, there will be very few students in our schools whose educational experience will not be a successful one.

Children with drug and alcohol exposure, like other children at risk for school difficulties, may present a number of problematic behaviors. Each child is unique, but certain characteristics appear among children most likely to have problems. The at-risk child will probably have one or more of the following traits:*

- Easily distracted.
- Limited problem-solving skills.
- Takes longer than other children to complete a task.
- Easily stimulated by other children or events inside or outside the classroom.
- Develops interactive and representational play skills later than other children.
- Difficulty understanding instructions or responding to commands.
- Limited range of facial expression (restricted affect).
- Problems with emotional attachments (is unable to develop strong attachments to teachers or peers, *or* attaches indiscriminately to others).
- Poor impulse control.
- Delayed in expressive and/or receptive language.
- Gross motor or fine motor coordination is not as developed as other children. May be awkward or clumsy.

Students with prenatal chemical exposure, like other children, will benefit from a learning environment that is consistent and structured, and that recognizes their individual learning and emotional needs. There will continue to be some students who have developmental delays or other needs that require specialized services. When teachers suspect problems of a serious nature, they should consult their school-based assessment team to set up an Individualized Educational Program (IEP).

* This list is adapted from the materials of the Los Angeles Unified School District (1989) and the Florida Department of Education (1989).

In cases where children present unique challenges, it may be necessary to make a referral to clinics or universities outside the school system. We do not expect that special cases like this will disappear when the teaching strategies we recommend here are implemented. However, we do expect that teachers and students will report greater success in the school experience, and that everyone will benefit.

What Are "Learning Styles"?

Learning styles have been defined as the "cognitive, conceptual, affective and behavioral patterns that are typical, consistent and stable processes which people use in their learning" (Guild and McKinney, n.d.). In simpler terms, these are the ways people handle new situations and information, and apply their experience and knowledge.

Most people who study learning believe an individual's learning style develops in combination with environmental factors and innate capabilities—that is, an interplay between nature and nurture. We know that children who come from home environments where they do not feel protected and provided for will often have difficulties in school and learning. Children who are encouraged to explore their environments may learn more easily. And a child's own biologically based strengths and weaknesses will also contribute to how that child learns.

Children's learning styles are not directly related to level of intelligence. A linear, analytic learner is not necessarily more intelligent than an auditory or kinesthetic learner. But the skills of the linear thinker are easier for schools to measure with the evaluation systems currently in place. This is why any child assessment must include a number of components designed to measure a wide range of approaches to learning, remembering and understanding information.

There are a variety of ways of categorizing how children learn. We offer some examples which are not exhaustive, but are some of the most common. They are included because they are descriptive, and because methods for teaching these learners are readily evident. Children may have a single, predominant style of learning, or may learn through several different styles.

Visual Learner

Characteristics: Sensory learning style. Child learns by *seeing* things, and describes information and experience in visual terms.

Example: Carol did well in arithmetic in first and second grade, but had problems in third grade. In reviewing the style of math instruction in these classes, it was discovered that Carol's first and second grade teachers had encouraged her to use counting blocks, but her third grade teacher did not use them. Carol was again given counting blocks, then was taught to imagine the number problems in her head.

Teaching strategies: Facilitate the child's ability to *see* the task at hand. Ask the child to show you what he or she is doing. Demonstrate new tasks. Use visual cues in questions and discussions: "Can you *see* what I'm talking about?" "Can you *show* me an example?" "Let's take a *look* at this problem."

Use visually oriented teaching materials: illustrated books, photographs, films or videos, diagrams, visual computer learning programs. Employ visual learning activities that build successful experiences in learning and emphasize the child's areas of strength (birdwatching for science class, comparing student heights in health class, painting and drawing, playing matching games).

Auditory Learner

Characteristics: Sensory learning style. Child learns by *hearing* things, and describes information and experience in auditory terms.

Example: When given a story to read to himself, John would read aloud, though quietly. Evaluation of his reading comprehension indicated that he understood much more when he heard the story.

Teaching strategies: Facilitate the child's ability to hear instructions or information about the task at hand. Use auditory cues in questions and discussions. "Can you *tell* me more about this exercise?" "Let's *talk* about this some more." When giving instructions or responding to questions, ask the child to "*listen* carefully" to what you say.

Use auditorily oriented teaching materials: cassette tapes of stories, films or videos with sound, music, computer learning programs with sound, voice-instruction and feedback. Employ auditory and sound-based learning activities that build successful experiences in learning and emphasize the child's areas of strength (music appreciation, word games that are spoken out loud, story telling, singing, listening with eyes closed, reading aloud).

Kinesthetic Learner

Characteristics: Sensory learning style. Child learns by *touching and feeling* things, and describes information and experience in kinesthetic terms.

Example: Kelso saw a volcano erupt on a news broadcast. He didn't quite understand the explanation provided by his teacher, but when the class built a volcano for their science class, Kelso came alive. He built the papier-mâché structure, helped stir the lava mixture, and so forth. When he watched a documentary film on volcanoes later, Kelso excitedly narrated the film, while the other students imitated volcano sounds. His hands-on experience had helped him understand the concepts.

Teaching strategies: Facilitate the child's ability to have hands-on experience in learning activities. Use kinesthetic cues in questions and discussions. "What does this *feel* like to you?" "Can you *move* your arm this way?" "Let's *touch* this and see what it *feels* like."

Use kinesthetically-oriented teaching materials: hands-on materials with a variety of textures, computer learning programs that use a joystick, mouse or trackball. Employ kinesthetic learning activities that build successful experiences in learning and emphasize the child's areas of strength (dance, sculpture, building or manipulating models, theater or roleplays).

Global Learner

Characteristics: Cognitive learning style. Child uses a *global* approach ("whole-to-part"), starting with a whole concept before breaking it down into its component parts.

Example: Cyrus always reads the end of the story first. He feels the need to know how things end before he can focus on the details of the story.

Teaching strategies: Facilitate the child's ability to see "the whole picture" before presenting details of the work. Use cues related to the larger task. "You will be able to read *the whole story* yourself after you have learned these new reading words." "You will be able to divide up the apples we are giving to the class when you can work out these math problems."

Use whole-language techniques that combine reading, writing and speaking. Global learners can work successfully with a wide range of materials and approaches. It is most important that the lesson be presented from a global perspective ("tell the whole story"), and that all materials needed for an exercise are available at its start. Global learners often enjoy external rewards (stickers, prizes) and do best with structured activities and regular feedback.

Analytic Learner

Characteristics: Cognitive learning style. Child uses an *analytic* approach ("part-to-whole"), starting with component parts and inferring a larger concept.

Example: In copying a set of designs, Joe counts the number of figures in each design and numbers each design as he draws it. When talking about a story he has read, he may focus more on the "trees" than on the "forest."

Teaching strategies: Many standard school curricula are already designed for the analytic learner. Facilitate the child's ability to start with details, then put them together in a complete project. Use cues related to development of the larger concept. "Now that you can read all the vocabulary words, lets *put them together* into the story." Analytic learners can also learn successfully with global teaching approaches.

Use techniques that move from specific to general concepts. Use a variety of teaching materials: interactive video or computer programs that provide direct feedback, books and written materials, films. Analytic learners often enjoy less personal teaching strategies, such as lectures or reading assignments, and activities that allow them to process information independently.

Putting It All Together: What Does the Classroom Look Like?

The Los Angeles Unified School District (1989) and the Florida Department of Education (1989) have adopted curricula designed to meet the needs of children with substance exposure. These curricula offer guidelines and teaching strategies in the areas of learning behaviors, play, social and emotional development, communication skills, motor skills, and the implementation of home-school partnerships.

A careful reading of the curricula indicates that guidelines are for use with "at risk" students generally; children with prenatal chemical exposure are but one component of this group. The guidelines include the following recommendations:

- Limit the number of objects in the classroom. Bring out sets of objects or learning materials as needed. Reduce stimuli for the easily distracted student.
- Establish stable routines in the classroom. Keep transitions to a minimum, and attend to transitions carefully (give students a few minutes' warning before a transition is made, for example).
- Recognize the range of developmental levels among children in the class. Develop teaching activities accordingly.
- Provide information in a variety of ways when instructing children in new concepts or activities. Include visual, auditory and tactile instructions.
- Model appropriate social and learning behaviors for children.
- Build successful experiences for all learners. Identify and acknowledge each child's unique capabilities.
- Monitor students' developmental progress and arrange formal developmental assessments as needed.
- Respond with encouragement and alternative strategies if necessary when a child initially attempts a new or difficult activity.
- Identify family factors that can help students succeed in school (for example: a parent's emphasis on the importance of education, family concern for a child's welfare and happiness, parents' expertise as observers of their own children).

Multimodal Teaching Techniques

The ability to work with a variety of learning styles in a single classroom or other setting involves a *multimodal teaching approach.* There are practical ways to adapt and modify lessons to provide multimodal instruction. These adaptations may affect the overall appearance of a classroom, the schedule of the school day, or the ways students interact with teachers and with one another.

In the following section, we present a set of six suggestions for instruction of children at risk for school failure. These are recommendations for children who learn in non-analytic ways, but do not diminish the ability of the analytic learner to benefit from the lessons. The goal is to establish an environment that respects a wide variety of learning styles—school that works for everybody! *

1. Help create a positive environment in class, one in which students help one another.

- ❧ Use small group work in lessons, or have students work with partners.
- ❧ Use cooperative learning activities, or combine students into teams for games and competitions.
- ❧ Encourage positive "school spirit" or classroom attachment.
- ❧ Have established groundrules which guide students to respect one another. Respond to incidents of teasing, hazing, racial or ethnic remarks, or other emotional attacks promptly. Be clear with students that behavior and comments of this nature are inappropriate and unacceptable in the classroom and on the playground.
- ❧ Provide generous positive reinforcement, praise and compliments. Minimize criticism. Do not embarrass students in front of classmates.
- ❧ Encourage students to be helpful to one another, and give them opportunities to talk about ways they have helped others outside the classroom.

2. Make the content personal.

- ❧ Use teaching examples from the students' lives, school events or your own personal experience. Learning should be personal as well as academic.

* These suggestions are adapted from material developed by Guild and McKinney (n.d.), and we are substantially indebted to them for the content of this section.

- Use roleplays, theater and performance, simulations.
- Provide information about the personal lives of people studied in class (scientists, historical figures, composers). Help the students see them as "real people."
- Use examples familiar to students: money problems, baseball statistics.
- Encourage students to develop and express their own opinions about lessons. Create a class setting where individual opinions are respected.

3. Present learning in a global way.

- Give an overview of the lesson and review the main concept before discussing details.
- Talk through the steps of a project before beginning.
- Review relevant past lessons before beginning new learning.
- Give an example before giving a definition.
- Encourage children to skim through a reading, looking at captions, illustrations or headings, before beginning in earnest.
- Give students a clear sense of beginnings and endings (of a math problem, of a story, of a piece of music).

4. Make connections that highlight the relevance of the lesson.

- Present lessons with common themes. If the health lesson talks about family relationships, the math lesson can include story problems about numbers of people in a family.
- Use local history, school or family events, popular music, etc., in learning tasks (have students write a family history, for example, or do math lessons based on the price of tickets to see a popular performer).
- Use students' own work as examples (in the art lesson, students could illustrate their own stories; for reading, students could dictate stories to the teacher which are bound together for a reading book).
- Make connections between classroom work and the work in textbooks. Do not assume students will understand these are related.

5. Provide a context for learning and a rationale for the lesson.

- Review the purpose of the lesson, and repeat it when an example from the lesson makes it clear.
- Help students see and discuss ways new learning will be relevant to their current lives.
- Use metaphors, analogies and other images to help students understand the context and rationale of the lesson. ("If you're going to sing a song at a concert, you need to memorize all the words. If you're going to succeed in math, you need to memorize the multiplication tables.")
- Use students' own work or examples from their own lives in lessons.

6. Provide structure. Be clear in expectations and directions. Be organized.

- Provide short, written outlines of the lesson. Review the lesson sequence several times, including the particular point of review the class is at.
- Maintain regular classroom schedules. Keep a schedule posted.
- Have a clear system through which students get regular feedback on their performance and progress. Be available for questions about student performance.
- Return assignments quickly with corrections and feedback.
- Have lesson materials and supplies ready and available when needed.

When Resources Are Limited: Practical Suggestions

Even with a limited (or non-existent) budget, teachers can begin to create classrooms that offer support for multimodal teaching. Here are some steps taken by teachers working with a multimodal approach, many of which cost little or nothing to implement.

- "I've simplified the appearance of my classroom. It used to be very busy, with drawings and pictures everywhere. We had even strung wires across the room so there were more places to hang things. Now, I have one wall with student pictures on it, and a very simple bulletin board with a calendar, the daily schedule and one item related to a current lesson. I keep the blackboard blank unless we're actually working on it. The students who are easily distracted are able to concentrate on their work more in this classroom."

- "I've pulled together lots of little items I can use for math and science learning. I use cardboard egg cartons for all kinds of things—the students can make sets of colored scraps of paper by putting them into the egg slots. I save the plastic canisters from film and the students play memory and math games with these. We collect science specimens and keep them available in glass jars. We have a great sense of discovery in our class with some of the simplest things!"
- "We play music during art activities. I have a good selection of 'quiet music' that seems to calm the children down."
- "I make sure I have at least one independent meeting with each student every week. I have 32 students, so this is not easy to schedule. But for a lot of my kids, just five minutes of one-to-one time with me takes them a long way. If the whole class is working on projects or reading, I'll have time to talk with one or two students. We keep weekly records of their work and progress, and the children are very adept at commenting on their own strengths and shortcomings. They participate actively in evaluating how they're doing, and they take a lot of responsibility for their success."
- "I have students with a lot of different strengths and weaknesses. For the children who are more likely to be identified as 'poor learners,' who learn in non-analytic ways, I make a special effort to reinforce areas of competence. Then I give them an opportunity to demonstrate their competence to the rest of the class. A couple of students are great dancers, so they did a special performance for the class. One student likes fishing with his grandfather, and I invited him and his grandfather to give the class a fishing lesson—everyone made fishing poles out of cardboard and string, and we went out on the playground and practiced casting. Children who started out the year insecure and unmotivated have blossomed with this kind of attention and respect."
- "I used to have the desks in my classes set up in standard rows. Most of the children spent the day looking at another student's back. Now, I've

set the desks up in groups of four, facing each other, and the students are able to look at one another, interact, learn from each other. Each group is a team, and they collaborate on certain class projects. I've tried to mix students with different learning styles in each team, and we work on projects that require different ways of thinking so that all the students' talents are called into play."

Guidelines for Teachers: Making Change Possible

If teachers are not familiar with the practical applications of learning theory, it may seem a challenging task to begin to implement so many suggestions all at once. It is possible, of course, to bring these applications in a few steps at a time. Most teachers report that multimodal teaching gets easier over time. Ideas that used to take a long time coming appear with sudden flashes of insight, and teaching that once seemed difficult becomes easy as it becomes familiar.

We suggest a multimodal teaching approach because it will benefit at-risk students, including children with drug and alcohol exposure, but this kind of teaching is also rewarding for teachers. As children begin to succeed more, teaching becomes more gratifying. Children who are involved more actively in their learning are more interesting to work with, and new discoveries take place for teacher and student alike. It *does* take some extra effort to teach in this way. Most teachers find the rewards make this worthwhile.

It is important for teachers shifting to a multimodal teaching approach to build in positive reinforcement for themselves for the extra effort they are making. We offer the following general suggestions in support of the teacher's task:

- Remember your own learning styles. Use your favorable learning experiences as a starting point when you plan lessons. Then consider how children who learn differently from you can benefit from your teaching as well.
- Meet with parents or caregivers at the beginning of the school year and discuss their views on their children's learning style. Parents have considerable insight about their children's areas of strength, and you may be able to establish a good alliance with parents if they see you are interested in their children's competence rather than their limitations.

- Consult with other teachers and class aides to share ideas, successes and failures in multimodal teaching.
- Conduct informal assessments of your students by asking yourself regularly, "Who is struggling or succeeding with which kinds of tasks? What kind of teaching is most successful with my students?"
- Reframe student behaviors. Is that child hyperactive, or does he need to move to learn? Is this girl noisy, or is she an auditory learner? Reframing can help us see new strategies and solutions.
- Enjoy the adventure of designing a multimodal classroom—one that is flexible enough for the visual, the auditory, the global, the analytic and the kinesthetic learner.
- Remember that the global (whole to part) approach is successful with all students, but that each student will require modifications for his or her particular learning needs.
- Create an environment of excitement, where learning—and teaching—is fun.
- Let your students know how valuable they are and how much you believe in their ability to learn.
- If learning issues occur that are challenging for you, or for which you might need consultation, call in members of your multidisciplinary school team for discussion and evaluation as needed.

Teaching Based on Learning Styles: Does It Work?

"I am an educational specialist who works with children whose learning styles are often not well-addressed by traditional teaching methods and curricula. I work directly with children, teach pediatricians and other medical personnel about children's learning styles, and run a teaching clinic for teachers.

"An example from one of my remediation sessions shows how easy it can be to design individualized programs for children once you know how they learn. One of my groups has three students. The first is an active kinesthetic learner, the second is more logical and analytic, and the third learns auditorily.

"They were all to work on a math task where they learned about 'sets.' I provided objects for the kinesthetic learner to manipulate. First, I showed her the concept by using those objects, grouping them in various ways. I allowed her to ask questions. Then she used the objects to create sets of her own that she could see and feel. The concept became clear to her. In the next few weeks, she'll begin to read about this concept in books, and she'll be able to recognize what the books are describing.

"The second student had more of a logical, analytic learning style. For him, I provided reading materials that described the math concept. However, I had noticed he had some visual memory problems. So I had him read about the concept in several different books and do paper and pencil problems that he repeated until he reached 100 percent mastery.

"My auditory learner used to get in trouble for talking in class. He was always muttering under his breath, and his teacher complained that he seemed to be talking to himself. He was! He needed to repeat things to himself continuously to learn. For this math task, he used a computerized program that provided voice simulation to talk him through the steps of each problem and gave him immediate feedback about how he was doing. 'That's right!' the computer would say to him. Or, 'Try again.'

"These types of learning styles are pretty common. They're not new or different. But it seems that teacher training hasn't caught up with the real world quite yet. And some kids are getting a rotten deal because of it."

—Special education teacher

In the spring of 1989, the Office for Academic Achievement in Seattle began an interesting experiment. First, they conducted assessments of elementary students. Next, based on scores from a number of measures, each child was placed in one of three categories: low, average or high achiever.

The office then tested students among the group of low achievers to determine their learning styles. They found that this sample of children, predominantly children of color, was more likely to include field dependent (global) learners than field independent (analytic) learners. These were students who learned best when given a whole concept that was then broken down into its component parts.

Previous research had already indicated that global and analytic learning styles were not correlated with levels of intelligence. It was possible, therefore, that some of the "low achievers" were actually students who had academic strengths that were being overlooked by the educational system.

The students' teachers were trained in techniques for teaching the global learner and encouraged to apply these techniques in their classes. As the students received education more appropriate to their learning styles, they began to improve their school performance. In the schools that best implemented instructional techniques suited to the learning styles of the students, improvement in test scores was greatest. In the course of this three year project, it is expected that these gains will continue.

In large classrooms, teachers can create projects that are global in nature and combine teaching strategies suited to the variety of learners who may be in the classroom. For example, Kelso's experience with the volcano, described earlier, actually contained a number of teaching approaches (the teacher described volcanoes, a model provided hands-on experiential learning, a film offered visual and auditory information, the student's narration of the film provided further auditory information). The students explored the visual and auditory aspects of volcanoes, became excited about learning why volcanoes act as they do, and were able to watch step-by-step how a volcano forms and becomes active.

Teachers can set up learning centers in a classroom that focus on particular sensory areas. No center has a solitary focus—they all overlap somewhat. But a tactile center could allow the exploration of textures and be related to science lessons. A visual center might have match-up designs, mazes, pictures and puzzles. An auditory center could have music, poetry, books on tape, computer activities with voice feedback, and so forth. All the necessary materials to complete specific assignments would be available at the appropriate learning center. Global and analytic learners would both be able to approach the task in the method most comfortable and useful for them.

> "Children in my classroom seem to fall into three or four learning styles. I try to design activities that reach at least twenty-five percent of my students at any one time. And I try to incorporate all learning styles over the course of a lesson. So there may be times when children are working outside their area of strength for a while, but never for very long."
>
> —Teacher

Children with prenatal drug or alcohol exposure are at risk for academic difficulties and school failure. Yet experience and research have shown that all children can learn, and that when teaching strategies take a child's learning style into consideration, most children can experience academic success.

The success of these and other at-risk children depends in large part on the ability of individual teachers and entire school systems to make a commitment to students: that each child has learning potential, that the child's failure is also the school's failure, and that the school will not let the child fail.

❧ ❧ ❧

Shara
A Charming Girl with Severe Learning Problems

Shara was a ten-year-old girl who had been living with her mother for the past year. Shara's mother, Florence, had used heroin and alcohol during her pregnancy, and had continued using for many years after Shara's birth. As a very young child, Shara had lived in foster homes, and between the ages of six and nine she had lived with her grandmother.

Florence had completed a heroin treatment program and was active in Narcotics Anonymous. She had been successful living a drug- and alcohol-free lifestyle over the past two years, and had been awarded legal custody of Shara. She and Shara had established a loving, friendly relationship, and she cared about her daughter very much.

Florence was concerned about Shara's school performance, however. Her daughter had been enrolled in regular education classes from kindergarten through second grade, but had had significant difficulties keeping up with the class curriculum. In third grade, she had been moved into a complete special education program, but in the middle of fourth grade she was still having trouble with her lessons. Her teacher felt she was capable of doing the work, but was not motivated enough to apply herself. Shara herself enjoyed her classmates immensely, but disliked schoolwork and all subjects taught in her class, including art, music and dance.

Florence was aware that Shara had more trouble than most children remembering things. Her self-care skills were very poor. She was unable to brush her teeth, bathe or dress herself, and despite her mother's patient review of these tasks Shara seemed to repeatedly forget all she had been taught.

Florence asked the school to arrange an evaluation of Shara's learning performance. The school, noting Shara was significantly behind in all academic skills and was not succeeding in her special education program, agreed. She was evaluated by the school psychologist, a speech and language specialist, and a neurologist.

Findings: The neurologist found that Shara had an awkward gait, poor fine motor skills, small head circumference, and showed signs suggestive of neurologic immaturities.

The speech and language specialist indicated that Shara used words and language in the manner of a much younger child. The girl was, however, social and easy to understand. She used colloquialisms similar to those of her mother, and Black English typical of her local community.

The psychologist found Shara to be a charming girl with an attractive personality. She was quite talkative and asked many questions—"Am I pretty? Do you like my earrings? How do you use this pencil? What's your name?" The psychologist evaluated Shara and found her to be mildly retarded in all areas. Her verbal reasoning, visual reasoning and quantitative skills were all well below norms for her age. Shara's memory skills were weakest, especially visual memory, and she had considerable difficulty with sequencing skills.

The psychologist further evaluated Shara's development, focusing on her communication and self-care skills. These findings showed that Shara's performance was more like that of a normal five year old than a fourth grader.

In a team discussion, all of the evaluators also noted that Shara had wide-set small eyes, drooping eyelids, a small head and an underdeveloped philtrum. These features are associated with Fetal Alcohol Syndrome, and Shara's mother was known to have used alcohol during her pregnancy. A referral was made to a genetics clinic for further evaluation.

Outcome: The genetics clinic confirmed a diagnosis of Fetal Alcohol Syndrome for Shara. Shara's mother was put in contact with a state-funded regional center providing services for mentally retarded children. They were able to arrange some special training for Shara in self-care. Florence herself was referred to a class for parents of retarded children, which would help her have more realistic expectations about Shara's capabilities. The parenting class also helped parents develop behavior management skills that were useful in caring for retarded children.

The regional center's program helped Shara with several of her self-care skills by breaking them down into individual steps, taking Polaroid snapshots of each step, and posting the pictures where the girl could follow them as she completed a task. She needed extremely detailed help for such tasks. For example, brushing her teeth worked out to a 17-step process: (1) walk into the bathroom, (2) open the cabinet, (3) take out the toothpaste, (4) take out the toothbrush, (5) remove the cap from the toothpaste, and so on.

The school arranged a new Individualized Educational Program (IEP) conference. The additional information on Shara made it clear that the girl would have significant limitations as she matured, and could not be expected to succeed in an academically oriented program. However, Shara had excellent social skills—so good, in fact, that people (including her fourth grade teacher) tended to be fooled into assuming she was capable of much more than she accomplished.

A decision was made to place Shara in a special program for children with mild mental retardation. The program emphasized daily living skills, basic academics and prevocational training. Over her school years, Shara would develop some basic job skills that would help her live somewhat independently in her adult years.

Follow-up: Shara is now in fifth grade and is fully integrated into her special program. She seems happier, and for the first time in her life describes learning as "fun." She takes a lot of pride in her new accomplishments—she can brush her teeth, wash and dress herself, and help with the dishes at home. The system of visual prompting with Polaroid snapshots continues to be used, both at home and school, and as Shara's skills on a particular task improve she can sometimes complete it with fewer visual prompts. She can now brush her teeth, for example, guided by only eight photos.

Her mother and her school have been very supportive of these efforts and of the adjustments Shara has needed to make in her new program.

Comment: *Shara's experiences are similar to those of the small percentage of children with substance exposure who will suffer severe effects from their mothers' substance use. Children with problems as significant as Shara's will need special attention in school and community activities.*

Even for the small proportion of children severely affected by prenatal chemical exposure, careful evaluation and thoughtful planning will usually improve the situation. Shara will probably not be able to live an independent life as an adult, but she will have some self-care and social capabilities that give her a sense of self-worth. She is expected to be able to develop skills that can allow her to contribute in some way to her community.

❧ ❧ ❧

Chapter 10

Policy Planning and a Look to the Future

The great majority of providers working with children are out on the front lines, offering a focused kind of service in a specific setting. They are teachers teaching one grade in one school; social workers coordinating services for thirty families in one community; nurses helping pediatric patients in one clinic.

Front-line providers do not usually have the opportunity to establish broad-ranging policies affecting children and their families. Yet, in this book designed primarily for front-line providers, we felt it was essential to include some policy recommendations addressing the needs of children with chemical exposure and drug- and alcohol-involved families.

We do this because we believe front-line providers have opinions about policy, certainly have expertise relevant to the development and implementation of policy, and can influence the setting of policy. When you believe in something strongly, you can express that belief in talks with administrators, discussions with colleagues, communications to elected representatives, letters to the editors of newspapers and magazines, and interactions with members of the community you serve.

Specific Recommendations

We have made a number of recommendations throughout this book. We believe absolutely that as providers we all must advocate for our students, clients and patients, and for the children in our communities, as much as possible. We hope you agree, and that the following list is useful in clarifying some of the issues of particular importance to children with drug and alcohol exposure and their families.

- Children have individual strengths and deficits. Avoid making broad generalizations about children with chemical exposure and look at each child individually, identifying strengths and helping the child compensate for weaknesses.
- Families of children with chemical exposure, especially those that are drug- and alcohol-involved, will usually need services from a variety of agencies and providers. Provisions should be made to offer and coordinate this kind of multiservice care. Ideally, in neighborhoods with

high levels of drug or alcohol use, family centers will be established where many services are available in one location.

- The family is the most important influence on a child's development. The importance of the family should be emphasized in interactions with caregivers. Wherever possible, children should be placed in the custody of families of origin (except when doing so would endanger the child's well-being).
- Chemical dependency is a medical problem and should be treated medically. Punitive legal measures applied to pregnant women or new mothers who have used drugs or alcohol during pregnancy will ultimately cause more damage than good and should be avoided.
- There is a great need for more treatment and recovery programs. Funding should be provided for the establishment of more programs. A variety of program approaches should be available because different approaches will be successful with different people.
- There is a particular need for treatment and recovery programs that serve pregnant women, adolescent pregnant women, women with children, couples and families. More residential programs that provide beds for children should be funded.
- Broad-based prevention education about drug and alcohol abuse should be implemented in schools and community agencies. Children should be involved in prevention programs from a very early age.
- Infants or children known or suspected of having drug exposure should be carefully evaluated. If a child shows significant developmental, social or behavioral difficulties, therapeutic nursery programs should be considered.
- More funding should be provided for the establishment of therapeutic nursery programs.
- Schools and other service agencies should avoid labeling children as "drug exposed" except where there is a specific clinical benefit to such labeling (in a medical setting, for example, or in formal developmental assessment).
- Teachers and other providers involved in educating children should use a variety of approaches to teaching and employ theories about learning

styles in planning lessons and curricula. Children should have an opportunity to have successful experiences in school and other settings.

- Trainings that explain more about the problems of children with chemical exposure, give practical suggestions for working with children who have a variety of learning styles, and offer support for skill building should be offered to teachers and other providers.
- While the problem of prenatal substance exposure is an extremely dangerous one, providers and communities should maintain a sense of hope for children and for the future. There are programs which have been successful in helping children with chemical exposure catch up in many areas of development. There are also programs which have helped women of childbearing age achieve sobriety and recovery and stop using substances. Prevention efforts and education seem to be having some effect on the drug epidemic, including drug use by pregnant women. We can help improve this situation, and should not give up in our efforts to do so.

Broader Issues

In the area of policy planning, we must remember that substance use increases where people experience poverty, undereducation, unemployment, crime and violence. These conditions contribute to feelings of hopelessness and despair that make substance use seem easy and recovery seem impossible. For drug and alcohol abuse prevention to be truly successful, we must offer people hopeful alternatives: good schooling, safe communities and life-sustaining jobs. Providers working with children must try, to the fullest extent that we can, to influence these broad policy issues as well.

In the Future

We are encouraged by recent reports that the crack cocaine epidemic is slowing down in some areas, and that the number of babies born cocaine exposed may be on the decline. We must remain alert, however, to the continuing problems of prenatal substance exposure and avoid complacency when we hear reassuring information about decreased levels of drug use.

Other substances are being used with considerable frequency, crack cocaine is still in use by many people, and some regions are seeing a growth, not a slowing down, of crack and other drug use.

The broader problem of substance use and abuse will continue to endanger children prenatally. The complex dynamics of drug- and alcohol-involved families will affect children in many different ways as they grow and develop. Communities will continue to be devastated by the effects of the drug epidemic and alcoholism.

Prevention education can work, however. One of our major tasks is to support children today in developing drug-free lifestyles. We must help them understand moderation in the use of the legal drug alcohol. We can provide guidance that may help a young person determine whether he or she has problems with alcohol long before reaching a progressed stage of dependency.

We can also help children understand more about family issues in chemical dependency and give them tools they can use to escape the multigenerational cycles of dependency and addiction. We can offer them opportunities to build self-esteem and self-worth, feelings of competence and self-efficacy, and cultural and personal pride. We can emphasize the visibility of role models who are proud and confident and drug free—popular singers, sports stars, movie and television personalities.

We are not helpless in the face of this situation. There is much we can do to help the child with substance exposure today, and to improve the situation in the future. We cannot predict with certainty what the future will bring, but we can make a commitment to remain dedicated and energetic in our efforts to help children.

Appendix A

Background Information About Abusable Substances

Terms Used in This Appendix

CNS—Central nervous system. The brain and spinal cord.

Dependence—Physical dependence arises when the body adapts physiologically to the chronic use of a substance, such that when use is suddenly decreased or terminated, physical symptoms result (withdrawal). Psychological dependence arises when a user needs a substance to reach his or her maximum level of functioning, or is unable to reach a feeling of well-being without it.

OBS—Organic brain syndrome. Characterized by confusion, memory problems, disorientation, decreased intellectual functioning. Caused by chemical effects, infection, disease process or injury. In terms of substance use, OBS is the result of substance effects or secondary infections related to substance use.

Toxicity—Effects of a substance taken in quantities beyond a person's tolerance; overdose reactions. Any substance, used in excess, can cause toxic reactions.

Withdrawal—Symptoms and complications that arise from sudden decrease or termination of substance use after a dependency is established. Withdrawal from drugs that cause physical dependency may be life threatening.

Alcohol

Common or street names—Juice, brew.

Drug type—CNS depressant.

Dependence—Marked physical and psychological dependence.

Toxicity—Respiratory depression, respiratory arrest, coma, death.

Route of administration—Liquid is swallowed.

Subjective reports of effect—Relaxation, sociability, disinhibition, "helps me express my emotions," "fun," "tastes good."

Physical/CNS effects—Incoordination, impaired judgment, frequent urination, nausea, vomiting, slurring of speech, distortions of thought and memory.

Psychological/behavioral effects—Emotional lability (mood swings), sadness, anxiety, irritability, insomnia, aggressiveness, disinhibition, talkativeness.

Health problems—Injuries (including fatal auto accidents), hangovers, ulcer disease, gastritis, pancreatitis, increased susceptibility to hepatitis, cirrhosis, increased risk of some cancers, deterioration of peripheral nerves, temporary and permanent OBS, circulation problems.

Withdrawal—Agitation, tremors, cramps, insomnia, exhaustion, increased reflexes, nausea, vomiting, frightening hallucinations, delirium, heart failure, death.

Amphetamines

Common or street names—Brownies, whites, crank, black beauties, crystal, ice, uppers, speed, meth.

Drug type—CNS stimulant.

Examples—Methedrine (methamphetamine), Dexedrine, Benzedrine.

Dependence—High potential for psychological dependence. No significant physical dependence.

Toxicity—Psychotic-like behavior, paranoia, suicidal behavior, unconsciousness, awake but unable to talk for hours or days, rapid pulse, increased respiratory rate, markedly elevated blood pressure, very high body temperature, grand mal seizures, cardiovascular shock, cardiac arrhythmia, muscle rigidity, delirium, agitation, death.

Route of administration—Oral (pills), injection, smoked.

Subjective reports of effect—Exciting, energizing, decreases appetite, relieves sadness and depression, increases attentiveness, builds confidence, increases sexual pleasure.

Physical/CNS effects—Increased respiration, headaches, appetite reduction, restlessness, delirium, dizziness, pupils dilate, tremors, increased sweating, increased blood pressure, cardiac arrhythmias, auditory hallucinations.

Psychological/behavioral effects—Overactivity, confusion, mania, belligerence, suspiciousness, increased talkativeness, delusions, paranoia, euphoria, suicidal behavior, exhaustion, marked impairment of judgment.

Health problems—Possibility of precipitating schizophrenic break, injuries related to suicide attempts, injuries or accidents related to poor judgment, injuries related to marked belligerence (provoking fights), brain damage, physical exhaustion, general decreased resistance to infection because of poor nutrition and exhaustion, skin problems (self-imposed scratches related to sensations of "bugs crawling under my skin").

Injection users may suffer health effects related to poor needle hygiene and needle sharing, including severe vascular injuries; abscesses; infections, such as hepatitis, tetanus, or HIV; infections of the heart (endocarditis) and other organs.

Amphetamines are commonly used in combination with other drugs, including alcohol, heroin, methadone and barbiturates. Polydrug use increases medical complications and lethality.

Withdrawal—Lethargy, suicidal behavior (sometimes lasting several weeks), paranoia, psychosis, severe depression, abdominal cramping, asthma-like symptoms.

Cocaine

Common or street names—Coke, girl, snow, crack, her, lady snow.

Drug type—CNS stimulant.

Dependence—High potential for psychological dependence. No significant physical dependence.

Toxicity—Psychosis and paranoia, rapid pulse, increased respiratory rate, markedly elevated blood pressure, very high body temperature, grand mal seizures, cardiovascular shock, cardiac arrhythmia, heart attack, muscle rigidity, delirium, agitation, death.

Route of administration—Snorting, smoking, injection under skin ("skin popping"), intravenous injection.

Subjective reports of effect—Intense euphoria, sexual stimulation, increased sexual pleasure, loss of appetite, increased energy, increased confidence, sense of greater physical strength.

Physical/CNS effects—Increased respiration, headaches, appetite reduction, restlessness, delirium, dizziness, dilated pupils, tremors, increased sweating, increased blood pressure, cardiac arrhythmias, auditory hallucinations, seizures, strokes.

Psychological/behavioral effects—Restlessness, dizziness, increased talkativeness, irritability, insomnia.

Health problems—Malnutrition; apparent signs of stroke; bronchitis (especially for smokers); high blood pressure and associated intracranial hemorrhage; cardiac fibrillation; respiratory arrest; heart attack; destruction of nasal septum (for snorters); dental problems (from grinding of teeth during use); diminished blood supply to teeth, fingers and toes, with attendant slow healing of injuries; skin problems (self-imposed scratches related to sensations of "bugs crawling under my skin"); physical exhaustion; general decreased resistance to infection because of poor nutrition and exhaustion.

Injection users may suffer health effects related to poor needle hygiene and needle sharing, including severe vascular injuries; abscesses; infections, such as hepatitis, tetanus, or HIV; infections of the heart (endocarditis) and other organs.

Withdrawal—Muscle aches and pains, intense craving for cocaine, agitation, depression, decrease in appetite, fatigue, insomnia, lethargy.

Heroin

Common or street names—Harry, junk, smack, him, horse, the white lady.

Drug type—Opiate.

Dependence—Physical and psychological dependence.

Toxicity—Increasing depression, slowed respiration, flushing and cyanosis (skin turns blue from lack of oxygen), respiratory failure, death.

Route of administration—Sniffing, smoking, injection under skin ("skin popping"), intravenous injection.

Subjective reports of effect—Intense euphoria, removes sense of fear and worry, relieves physical pain.

Physical/CNS effects—Respiratory depression, sedation, sleep, stupor, slowing of heart, pupils constrict, body warmth, constipation, vomiting, lowered blood pressure, nausea, lethargy.

Psychological/behavioral effects—Euphoria, confusion, poor concentration, sleepiness, "nodding" (stupor), reduced sex drive, low activity level, reduced aggressiveness, low response to physical pain.

Health problems—Main health dangers stem from possibility of overdose, involvement in criminal activities to pay for drug, social and motivational difficulties, and malnutrition. Injection users may suffer health effects related to poor needle hygiene and needle sharing, including severe vascular injuries; abscesses; infections, such as hepatitis, tetanus, or HIV; infections of the heart (endocarditis) and other organs.

Withdrawal—Yawning, watery eyes, nausea, vomiting, goose flesh, abdominal cramps, muscle spasms, anxiety, irritability, loss of appetite, pupils dilate, convulsions, and (rarely) coma and death.

LSD (lysergic acid diethylamide)

Common or street names —Acid, window pane.

Drug type—Hallucinogen.

Dependence—No physical dependence. Slight potential for psychological dependence.

Toxicity—Panic, flashbacks, confusion, convulsions, suicide attempts.

Route of administration—Oral (wafers, tablets, painted on stamps or stickers).

Subjective reports of effect—Euphoria, ability to have "new experiences," "learn about inner self," "discover universal truths."

Physical/CNS effects—Altered perceptions; synesthesia (mingling of senses—"taste sounds, hear colors"); sense of timelessness, dreamy state; visual, auditory and tactile hallucinations; tachycardia; increased body temperature; chaotic disruption of thinking; markedly dilated pupils.

Psychological/behavioral effects—Paradoxic feeling states (happy and sad at same time, peaceful and anxious), panic reactions, feelings of depersonalization, lability of affect, hilarity, paranoia, feelings of profound understanding, "feels like floating," some prolonged psychotic reactions, inability to distinguish reality from fantasy.

Health problems—Some prolonged psychotic reactions, flashbacks, social difficulties in chronic users, loss of motivation, risk of accidents and injuries. Questions about chromosomal damage among users remain unresolved.

Withdrawal—None observed.

Marijuana

Common or street names—Pot, hemp, herb, loco, mota, joint, reefer, J.

Drug type—Cannabinoid.

Dependence—No physical dependence. Psychological dependence marked in some individuals.

Toxicity—Panic, anxiety, vomiting, nausea, psychotic reactions (in rare cases).

Route of administration—Smoked, swallowed (sometimes mixed with foods), snuffed, injected (rarely).

Subjective reports of effect—Relaxation; altered perceptions of touch, time and space; euphoria; lack of concern about current problems or the future; sociability; "fun."

Physical/CNS effects—Drowsiness, reddening of eyes, memory problems (especially sequencing), confusion about time (minutes may seem like hours), incoordination, respiratory depression, depth perception may be impaired, appetite increases, visual recovery from bright lights slow (may impair night driving).

Psychological/behavioral effects—Increased talkativeness; feeling of calm; euphoria; inappropriate and prolonged laughter; sense of sight, taste, touch intensified; poor judgment; incoordination; panic attacks (rare); pseudo-hallucinations (rare).

Health problems—Long-term memory problems; lung damage, with increased susceptibility to cough, hoarseness, bronchitis; possible increased risk for lung cancer with chronic use; possible fertility problems; lack of motivation and social difficulties; increased risk of injuries (including auto accidents).

Withdrawal—No signs noted.

Methadone

Note—Methadone is a very potent, highly addictive, dangerous opiate. It is prescribed in some heroin treatment programs because it can be taken orally, and the effects of withdrawal do not develop for about 24 hours after a dose is taken. This can help an intravenous heroin user to break the habit of needle use (which creates a high of its own), avoid criminal activity, minimize the anxiety-producing symptoms of withdrawal (which arise more quickly with heroin and other opiates), and move out of the social milieu of other users.

In methadone maintenance programs, the drug is provided at a level which "maintains" the user in a "normal" state, but does not provide a euphoric high. Theoretically, the individual's dosage of methadone will be gradually reduced until he or she is completely off opiates. In reality, many people continue to use methadone for years and are not successful at ending their dependence. Many methadone patients develop dependencies on other substances, including alcohol. Methadone is also used illicitly in some instances.

Drug type—Opiate (synthetic).

Dependence—High physical dependence. Psychological dependence.

Toxicity—Delirium, transient hallucinations, somnolence, death.

Route of administration—Oral (wafers or swallowed liquid).

Subjective reports of effect—Methadone is used illicitly primarily to assist in self-imposed efforts at heroin withdrawal, or to "boost" the effects of other drugs.

Physical/CNS effects—Similar to effects of other opiates, including heroin: sedation, respiratory depression, slowing of heart rate, decrease in blood pressure, constipation.

Psychological/behavioral effects—Similar to effects of other opiates, including heroin: euphoria, drowsiness, "nodding" (stupor), reduced sex drive, low activity level, low response to physical pain.

Health problems—Main health problem stems from danger of overdose in an individual who has not developed tolerance (including children who accidentally ingest the drug). Other long-term health effects seem to be minimal.

Withdrawal—Similar to other opiates, including heroin.

Minor Tranquilizers

Common or street names—Often based on color of pills. Reds, downers, nemmies, phenos, red devils, red and blues, seccy, yellow jackets, ludes.

Note—The "minor tranquilizers" include sleeping medications and antianxiety drugs. The "major tranquilizers" include antipsychotic drugs. Major tranquilizers are not CNS depressants and are rarely used to induce "highs."

Drug type—CNS depressant.

Examples—Barbiturates: Nembutal, Seconal, Amytal; Benzodiazepines: Librium, Valium, Xanax; Barbiturate-like drugs: Quaalude, Doriden.

Dependence—Physical and psychological dependence.

Toxicity—Psychosis, paranoia, hallucinations, unconsciousness, respiratory paralysis, serious drop in blood pressure, decreased cardiac functioning, coma, death.

Route of administration—Pills swallowed, intravenous injection (less common).

Subjective reports of effect—Calming, quieting, relaxing, euphoria, disinhibition. Some users report unpleasant feelings.

Physical/CNS effects—Anesthesia, decreased CNS function, decreased heart rate, decreased respiration, spinal cord depression, confusion, drop in blood pressure, sleepiness.

Psychological/behavioral effects—Quiet, slowed down, slurred speech, "drunk" in appearance, unsteady gait, poor judgment, stupor, psychosis, difficulty in thinking, disinhibition, quarrelsomeness.

Health problems—Major problem is development of physical dependency on drug with related dangers of withdrawal, and danger of overdose and death. There are over 3,000 deaths in the United States annually from barbiturate overdose. Many users are prescription users and have obtained the drug legally. Dangers may not be recognized. These drugs are commonly combined with narcotics, stimulants or alcohol, and in such combinations are especially life threatening.

Injection users may suffer health effects related to poor needle hygiene and needle sharing, including severe vascular injuries; abscesses; infections, such as hepatitis, tetanus, or HIV; infections of the heart (endocarditis) and other organs.

Withdrawal—Barbiturates: hyperexcitability, anxiety, confusion, disorientation, nausea, vomiting, cramps, delirium, increased reflexes, weakness, craving for drug, seizures. Benzodiazepines: headaches, anxiety, insomnia, tremor, fatigue, perceptual changes, tinnitus, sweating, decreases in concentration, delirium, psychotic features, seizures.

Phencycladine (PCP)

Common or street names—Angel dust, hog, Shermans.

Drug type—"Other." Does not fit in standard drug classes; shares properties with stimulants, depressants and hallucinogens. Originally developed as an animal tranquilizer.

Dependence—Mild physical dependence possible. Psychological dependence possible.

Toxicity—Numbness of extremities, mutism, confusion, coma, sweating and fever, markedly high blood pressure, convulsions, psychosis, catatonia, death. Toxic reactions tend to be longest-lasting of any abused drug.

Route of administration—Smoked, eaten, injected intravenously, sprayed on other substances (marijuana), snorted.

Subjective reports of effect—Provides an experience of an "out of the ordinary" state, new reality, expansion of sensations, increased strength.

Physical/CNS effects—Rise in blood pressure, heart rate, respiration, and reflexes; muscle rigidity; sweating; flushing; drooling; pupillary constriction; dizziness; incoordination; slurred speech; numbness of extremities; extreme impairment in ability to process sensory information.

Psychological/behavioral effects—Loss of sense of reality, dissolution of ego boundaries, emotional and intellectual disorganization, speech problems, disorientation, psychosis, depression, anxiety, confusion, behavioral outbursts, tantrums, assaultiveness, belligerence, hostility, unusual auto accidents, blank stare, gross incoordination, mood swings, suicidal gestures.

Health problems—After repeated exposures, drug effects may begin to occur chronically and memory gaps may appear. Major health problems are related to injuries, assaultiveness or suicidal behavior, as well as the risk of overdose.

Injection users may suffer health effects related to poor needle hygiene and needle sharing, including severe vascular injuries; abscesses; infections, such as hepatitis, tetanus, or HIV; infections of the heart (endocarditis) and other organs.

PCP is commonly used in combination with other drugs. Polydrug use increases medical complications and lethality.

Withdrawal—Withdrawal syndrome has not been confirmed. Continuing interest in obtaining the drug is common among persons who have ceased use, along with some discomfort and anxiety.

Solvent Inhalants

Common or street names—Glue, poppers, baggies.

Drug type—CNS depressant.

Examples—Gasoline, model glue, paint thinner, lighter fluid, nail polish remover, amyl nitrate.

Dependence—Little physical dependence. Psychological dependence.

Toxicity—Similar to alcohol and other CNS depressants, including delusions, visual hallucinations, excitement, coma, death.

Route of administration—Sniffing, inhalation (directly from container, or from cloth soaked with substance).

Subjective reports of effect—Exhilarating, "fun," forget troubles.

Physical/CNS effects—CNS depression, dizziness, disinhibition, loss of appetite, nausea and vomiting, increased salivation, incoordination, anorexia, ringing in ears, distorted perception of reality.

Psychological/behavioral effects—Aggressiveness, visual hallucinations, insomnia, bizarre behavior, depression, confusion, excitement, slurred speech.

Health problems—Impaired judgment can lead to accidents; some solvents may cause damage to bone marrow, liver, kidneys, brain; episodes of anoxia (lack of oxygen) during use can cause permanent brain damage and OBS; use of aerosol sprays can lead to sudden death.

Withdrawal—Temporary symptoms include delirium tremens, tremors, hallucinations, irritability.

Tobacco

Common or street names—Smoke, chew.

Drug type—Stimulant.

Dependence—Physical dependence in some individuals. Marked psychological dependence.

Toxicity—Paralysis of breathing, convulsions, death.

Route of administration—Smoked, chewed, snuffed.

Subjective reports of effect—Relaxation, stimulation, oral pacification, relieves constipation, "something to do with my hands," "keeps me from overeating," use responds to social reinforcement (seen as fun, sexy, successful, tough, etc.)

Physical/CNS effects—Stimulation followed by depression, increased heart rate, increased blood pressure, tremor and increased breathing at higher doses. Very high dose can lead to toxic reaction (especially a danger for young children).

Psychological/behavioral effects—Calms, relaxes.

Health problems—300,000 premature deaths are attributed to tobacco *annually* in the United States. Byproducts of tobacco include nicotine, carbon monoxide, ammonia, formaldehyde, phenols, creosote, antracen, and pyrene and hydrocyanic acids. May include arsenic and lead, due to insecticides used on tobacco plants.

Health effects include tremors; shortness of breath; nose and throat irritations; decreased ability to smell or taste; upper respiratory infections; chronic bronchitis; heart disease; cancers of mouth, larynx, esophagus and lungs.

Withdrawal—Irritability, anxiety, headaches, inability to concentrate, disruption of sleep, cramps, tremors, lethargy, hunger.

Appendix B

Effects of Substance Use on Pregnancy, Newborns and Children as They Grow

Substance use during pregnancy poses dangers to a developing fetus and can affect the child's growth and development. Dangers arise with the use of recreational substances as well as prescription and over-the-counter medications. Pregnant women should *always* check with their physicians before using prescription medications and read label inserts for over-the-counter drugs. Recreational substances, including alcohol, should be avoided throughout pregnancy.

The effects listed in the following tables demonstrate the range of possibilities for a variety of substances. Each pregnancy, and each child, will be different. In some cases, many of the listed complications will occur, and in others none of them will.

Research on some substances is incomplete. There may be other effects on pregnancy, fetal development, birth outcome and child development that are not yet established.

Alcohol		
Pregnancy Complications	**Neonatal Complications**	**Problems in Child Health or Development**
Miscarriage	Withdrawal	Mental retardation
Poor weight gain	Low birthweight	Developmental delay
Anemia	Restlessness	Learning disabilities
Hepatitis	Poor suck	CNS defects
		Heart disease
		Hearing problems
		Facial malformations
		Microcephaly (small head)
		Organ defects: muscles, bones, genitals
		Fetal alcohol syndrome*
		Fetal alcohol effect

* Fetal alcohol syndrome includes characteristic facial features, such as flattened nasal bridge, epicanthal folds, simple philtrum and thin lips.

Amphetamines		
Pregnancy Complications	**Neonatal Complications**	**Problems in Child Health or Development**
Prematurity	Low birth weight	Emotional problems
Poor weight gain		

Barbiturates

Pregnancy Complications	Neonatal Complications	Problems in Child Health or Development
Possible poor weight gain Psychosis	High pitched cry Irritability Disturbed sleep Tremors Restlessness Nervousness Hyperreflexia Weakness Vomiting Diarrhea Eating voraciously Skin rash	Birth defects

Cigarettes

Pregnancy Complications	Neonatal Complications	Problems in Child Health or Development
Miscarriage Prematurity Pre-eclampsia Placental abruption Placenta previa Slow intrauterine growth Difficulties conceiving	Low birth weight Increased risk of SIDS Increased neonatal mortality	Slow growth Learning disabilities Behavioral problems Respiratory disease during first five years (due to passive exposure to second-hand smoke)

Cocaine

Pregnancy Complications	Neonatal Complications	Problems in Child Health or Development
Prematurity Hypertension Tachycardia Placental abruption Precipitous delivery Poor nutrition Poor weight gain Slow intrauterine growth	Withdrawal Stroke Irritability Disturbed sleep Restlessness Hyperreflexia Poor feeding Microcephaly (small head)	Mental retardation Learning disabilities Behavior problems CNS defects Incoordination

LSD*

Pregnancy Complications	Neonatal Complications	Problems in Child Health or Development
Possible chromosomal damage	Possible chromosomal abnormalities	Some evidence of increased birth defects in laboratory animals

* Reports on LSD's effects on pregnancy and neonatal outcome are confounded by the prevalence of other drug use among users of LSD. Research findings concerning chromosomal damage in users have varied. If a mother or father *did* experience chromosomal damage, the problem could be passed on to children and result in birth defects.

Marijuana*

Pregnancy Complications	Neonatal Complications	Problems in Child Health or Development
Possible increase in loss of pregnancy (miscarriage, resorption)	Fetal exposure to THC (active ingredient in marijuana) through placenta; possible fetal effects	Some evidence of increased birth defects in laboratory animals

* Reports on marijuana's effects on pregnancy and neonatal outcome are confounded by the prevalence of other drug use among marijuana users. It has been a difficult to separate out the effects of marijuana over other drugs.

Opiates (Heroin, Methadone)		
Pregnancy Complications	**Neonatal Complications**	**Problems in Child Health or Development**
Prematurity Toxemia	Withdrawal High-pitched cry Irritability Fever Disturbed sleep Tremulousness Poor feeding Vomiting Diarrhea Increased risk of SIDS Major convulsive seizures	Developmental delay Learning disability Hyperactivity Vision problems Hearing problems Increased risk of SIDS

PCP (Phencycladine)		
Pregnancy Complications	**Neonatal Complications**	**Problems in Child Health or Development**
Injuries secondary to use of PCP	Jittery and tense Vomiting Diarrhea Poor reflex Nystagmus Fetal exposure to PCP through placenta; possible fetal effects	Poor attention span Possible birth defects

Appendix C

Tools for Assessing Development

Developmental assessments have two general purposes: (1) to determine and describe an individual child's areas of strength and weakness; and (2) to compare that child's rate of development to the skills we expect children to accomplish by certain age levels. At the time of this writing, there are no standardized developmental assessment tools designed specifically for children with drug and alcohol exposure.

We often lack specific information about the nature of prenatal chemical exposure—the dosage, the types of drugs used and in what combination, and the particular points of fetal development during which substances were used. Because of the wide variety of effects exposed newborns may experience, it would be difficult to design a single testing tool that would be useful or adequate in identifying such children or providing information about their strengths or deficits.

Instead, most providers experienced in developmental assessment (including psychologists, physicians, speech and language evaluators and learning specialists) will use measures already in general use. First, a general assessment is made of a newborn or infant using a screening measure (see the following section). If family or prenatal history or toxicology screens on mother or infant provide information about chemical exposure, this is noted as well. As the child grows and develops, the provider will select several different measures that can provide more detailed information about the particular strengths and weaknesses demonstrated on newborn screening and in continued general assessment. Usually a combination of assessments will be used because each tool emphasizes particular areas of development or skill. Reseach may in time indicate the strengths and weaknesses of these measures in assessing the development of drug exposed youngsters.

Until that time, the following measures are a sample of the evaluation tools used to determine the developmental status of infants, toddlers and school-age children. These are the most commonly used measures employed with children known or suspected to have prenatal chemical exposure.

Screening Measures

Denver Developmental Screening Test: This is a screening device to assess developmental delays in children between the ages of birth and six years. A developmental delay is scored if a child fails an item that 90 percent of children normally pass at a younger age. This measure assesses four behavioral areas: (1) personal-social, (2) fine motor adaptive, (3) language, and (4) gross motor. The Denver is widely used, in large part because it is well known and can be administered by nonprofessionals or non-specialists after brief training. It was not developed for use on premature or drug-exposed children, however, and was normed primarily on a middle class, Anglo population.

Neonatal Behavioral Assessment Scale: This measure, designed by T. Berry Brazelton, MD, evaluates the developmental status of children at birth. It can be administered by physicians, nurses or other trained professionals.

Cognitive Development

Bayley Scales of Infant Development: This measure, a standard in infant cognitive development, assesses the mental, motor and social development of children from birth to three years of age. The Bayley is currently being revised, and children with prenatal chemical exposure will be included in the standardization process. The revised measure is expected to be useful with such children.

Gesell Developmental Schedule: This measure was developed on the basis of results from longitudinal studies designed to assess normal development in infants and preschoolers. It generates information about the child's motor skills, adaptive behavior, language development and personal-social behaviors. This information is obtained through child observation and from data collected from the caretaker. The Gesell is most useful for identifying neurological and organically related deficits in children age four weeks through six years.

Kaufman Assessment Battery for Children: This individually administered measure of intelligence and academic achievement can be used with children between the ages of two and a half and twelve and a half. It includes scores for sequential processing, simultaneous processing, academic skills and nonverbal problem-solving skills. Interpretation for children in poverty is facilitated by the inclusion of norms which allow for adjustment based on parents' educational background and socioeconomic status. Norms are also available for African American children of varying socioeconomic backgrounds.

McCarthy Scales of Children's Abilities: This measure was designed for children between the ages of two and a half and eight and a half. It consists of 18 subtests that are grouped into six overlapping scales (verbal, quantitative, perceptual-performance, general cognitive ability, memory and motor). Because it includes a number of very easy items, it is particularly useful for assessing the strengths and weaknesses of mentally retarded children.

Miller Assessment for Preschoolers: This diagnostic tool for preschoolers was designed to assess development delays in a population of children between the ages of two years, nine months and five years, two months. It assesses preacademic foundations, motor coordination, verbal skills, nonverbal skills, and ability to learn and complete complex tasks. This measure also allows assessment of prenatal and early history, current medical and behavioral status and family history. The measure takes approximately 45 minutes to administer.

Mullen Scales of Early Learning (MSEL): This measure was structured to identify learning style, make suggestions for teaching, provide parents with information that can help them encourage their child's development, and link the child's assessment with family assessment. The MSEL assesses gross motor control and mobility, visual receptive organization and memory, speech and communication skills. The MSEL evaluates infants, toddlers and preschoolers from 15 to 68 months. It takes approximately 35 to 45 minutes to administer.

SOMPA (System of Multicultural Pluralistic Assessment): This measure was developed in 1979 in response to concerns about the misclassification of African American and Latino children as mentally retarded. A unique feature of this test is the integration of three components: (1) the Medical Component assesses physical health conditions that may affect the child's learning ability; (2) the Social System Component measures the child's social skills and adaptive behaviors; and (3) the Pluralistic Component evaluates the child's socio-cultural background. The battery includes a health history, child and parent/caretaker interviews, and the administration of standardized tests such as the Bender-Gestalt, the age appropriate Wechsler intelligence scale, and an assessment of children's adaptive behavior skills.

Stanford-Binet Intelligence Scale, Fourth Edition: This 1986 revision was based on a hierarchical model of general cognitive abilities. Designed to assess persons from age two to adulthood, it measures verbal reasoning, abstract/visual reasoning, quantitative reasoning and short-term memory skills. The model incorporates subtests in all four areas that represent the child's ability to solve problems through use of previously acquired skills and novel individual approaches. The Stanford-Binet can be used to assess the cognitive abilities of mainstream students who are having learning problems, to identify mental retardation and to identify intellectual giftedness.

Wechsler Intelligence Scales: Two tests used for preschool and school-age children are the Wechsler Preschool and Primary Scale of Intelligence—Revised (WPPSI-R) and the Wechsler Intelligence Scale for Children—III (WISC-III). The WPSSI is for children age two through six and a half, while the WISC-III was designed for children between the ages of six and sixteen. These are well-standardized measures that assess verbal skills (memory for previously learned information, word knowledge, knowledge of normative social behavior, mental computation) and performance skills (tasks of visual perception, hand-eye coordination, visual decoding). There are English and Spanish editions.

Speech and Language Development

Clinical Evaluation of Language Fundamentals—Revised: This measure includes several receptive and expressive language subtests that are used to provide information about the processing of language and its linguistic features.

Early Language Milestone Scale (ELMS): This test evaluates children between zero and thirty-six months in the areas of auditory expressive, auditory receptive, and visual skills. The clinician may elicit information through interview, incidental or direct observation.

Sequenced Inventory of Communication Development (SICD): The revised edition of this measure is designed to evaluate the language skills of young children between zero and five years. It is a screening tool that looks at a broad range of speech and language skills, assesses receptive and expressive communication skills and alerts the professional about the areas in which further indepth assessment is necessary. The scale can be completed by interviewing a parent/caregiver or directly observing the child. The factors measured by the scale are semantic, syntactic, pragmatic, perceptual and phonological factors. There are English and Spanish editions.

Learning Styles

Children's Embedded Figures Test: This test is an individually administered test designed to assess part-to-whole and whole-to-part learning styles. Children are required to find geometric forms that are hidden within pictures.

Slingerland Test for Identifying Children with Specific Learning Disabilities: The purpose of this measure is to identify students with specific learning disabilities. Each grade level of the test is designed to reveal the relative strengths and weaknesses that may exist in visual, auditory and sensory motor processing and functioning.

Swassing-Barbe Modiality Index (SBMI): This test assesses the elementary school child by looking at the sense modality through which the child most easily learns. The test is a matching-to-sample task for which the child is required to reproduce a stimulus item or sample.

Woodcock Johnson Reading Mastery: This is a comprehensive test battery with nine tests measuring reading ability in students from kindergarten through twelfth grade.

Kaufman Test of Educational Achievement: This is an individually administered measure of school achievement for children and adolescents in grades one through twelve which offers norms based on age and grade level for math application, reading decoding, spelling, reading comprehension and math computation.

Fine Motor Development

Beery Developmental Test of Visual Motor Integration: This measure assesses fine motor control and visual analysis skills. It has been normed on a number of racial and socioeconomic groups. This is an easier measure than the Bender-Gestalt for inexperienced examiners to use and interpret.

Bender Visual Motor Gestalt Test: This measure evaluates the child's ability to copy two-dimensional designs. It is used to assess visual motor integration skills. Children are expected to make no errors by the time they are twelve years of age. Errors after age twelve, as well as certain errors after age seven, are considered indicative of developmental delay or of the presence of organic factors that have negatively impacted visual processing.

Behavioral

Achenbach Child Behavior Checklist: This behavior checklist provides a profile of behavioral deviancy (eight or nine scales) and social competence (three scales) for children age four to sixteen. It provides standard scores on each scale (M=50, SD=10). The parent or the teacher may complete this measure; the interview takes approximately thirty minutes. Reliability and validity are satisfactory, scales are based on factor analytic findings.

Vineland Adaptive Behavior Scales: This interview measure is completed by the parent. It assesses communication skills (receptive, expressive, written), daily living skills (personal, domestic, community), socialization skills (interpersonal relationships, play and leisure time, coping skills), motor skills (gross and fine). Scores obtained on this measure can be used to compare the level of an individual child's adaptive skills with those of agemates in the standardization.

Research Tools

Howard University Developmental Assessment Profile (HUDAP): This measure was designed by the staff of Howard University Child Development Center to assess developmental status (fine and gross motor skills, adaptive behaviors, beginning language/ communication skills, and personal-social skills) in infants with substance exposure. Currently the measure is used for clinical and research purposes in the Child Development Center.

Lewis' Protocol: Developed by Keeta Lewis, a pediatric nurse in Napa, California, this recently developed (1989) measure was designed to assess the medical sequelae that may result from prenatal drug exposure. Assesses physical, motor and social behaviors of infants between zero and twelve months. The behaviors that are rated correspond to the clinical observations of medical staff who work with neonates and infants with chemical exposure.

Appendix D

Resources

This resource list provides information on a selection of available programs providing direct services to children affected by drugs or alcohol and to their families, training for professionals and foster parents, prevention programs, and coordination of available support services.

Some of these programs are quite new, and changes in address and telephone numbers may occur as they expand and grow. Local school multidisciplinary teams, county and university hospital child development departments, and city and state social service agencies (human resources, drug and alcohol, and mental health departments) can also provide evaluation, treatment and referral services.

Information Hotlines

Clearinghouse for Drug Exposed Children
(415) 476-9691
Information on community resources available for children with drug exposure, community education, newsletter. See additional listing for further description of services.

Cocaine Baby Help Line
(800) 638-BABY (Iowa, Ind., Ill., Wis., Mich., Minn.)
(312) 329-2512 (outside above areas)
Nursing helpline for caregivers of medically involved children with substance exposure.

Just Say No Kids Club
(800) 258-2766
(415) 939-6666
Prevention programs for seven to fourteen year olds.

National Clearinghouse for Alcohol and Drug Information
(301) 468-2600
(800) 729-6686
General resource for alcohol and drug information. See additional listing for further description of services.

Scott Newman Center
6255 Sunset Boulevard, Suite 1906
Los Angeles, CA 90028
(800)783-6396
Provide training tapes to organizations and publish a newsletter.

National Cocaine Hotline
(800) COCAINE
Information on drug treatment programs.

NIDA (National Institute on Drug Abuse) Hotline
(800) 662-HELP
General resource for alcohol and drug information.

Target Resource Center
(800) 366-6667
Drug abuse prevention programs for schools.

National Resource, Treatment and Training Programs

Al-Anon or Alateen
P.O. Box 182
Madison Square Station
New York, NY 10159-0182
Self-help groups for family and friends of alcoholics. Check local telephone listings for local groups.

Alcoholics Anonymous
P.O. Box 459
New York, NY 10163
Self-help groups for alcoholics. Check local telephone listings for local groups.

Askia Learning Products
P.O. Box 11538
Atlanta, GA 30310
(800) 635-3046
Computer programs and manipulative learning tools for students with non-analytic learning styles or learning disabilities.

Clearinghouse for Drug Exposed Children
Division of Behavioral and Developmental Pediatrics
University of California, San Francisco
400 Parnassus, Room A203
San Francisco, CA 94143-0314
(415) 476-9691
Child assessment, newsletter, research, teaching clinics, local and national resources for children with substance exposure and their families.

National Perinatal Resource Center
Office for Substance Abouse Prevention/Lewin ICF
(202) 842-2800
This resouce center will offer a broad range of services, including technical assistance for those designing and implementing services for drug affected children and families, coordinate national resource data, and publish a newsletter.

Family Welfare Research Group
University of California, Berkeley
School of Social Welfare
1950 Addison Street, Suite 104
Berkeley, CA 94704
(415) 643-7020
Multidisciplinary monograph on the effects of drug use on neonatal development and family functioning, assessment of drug treatment pro-

grams, and examination of relevant policy issues; training tapes; research.

Infant and Family Services Project
University of California, Los Angeles
1000 Veteran Avenue
23-10 Rehabilitation Center
Los Angeles, CA 90024-1797
(213) 825-9527
Model treatment programs, research.

Narcotics Anonymous
P.O. Box 9999
Van Nuys, CA 91409
Self-help groups for addicts. Check local telephone listings for local groups.

National Clearinghouse on Alcohol and Drug Information
P.O. Box 2345
Rockville, MD 20852
(301) 468-2600
(800) 729-6686
U.S. Federal clearinghouse for services and information on alcohol and other drugs. Largest, most comprehensive resource for alcohol and drug information in the world.

National Council on Alcoholism and Drug Dependence
12 West 21st Street
New York, NY 10010
(212) 206-6770
(800) NCA-CALL
Referral system connects callers to 200 nationwide affiliates engaged in alcohol and drug prevention education. Public policy office monitors legislation.

National Perinatal Resource Center
Office for Substance Abuse Prevention/ Lewin ICF
1090 Vermont Avenue NW, Suite 700
Washington, DC 20005
(202) 842-2800
Technical assistance for those designing and implementing services for children and families; newsletter; national resource data coordination.

Scott Newman Center
6255 Sunset Boulevard, Suite 1906
Los Angeles, CA 90028
(800) 783-6396
Newsletter (*All Babies Count*), media campaign to reduce sensationalist reporting on children with drug exposure.

Selected State and Local Organizations

California

Healthy Infant Program
Highland Hospital
1411 East 31st Street
Oakland, CA 94602
(415) 532-7722
Parenting programs for mothers recovering from addiction, child developmental assessment.

Mandela House
P.O. Box 19182
Oakland, CA 94619
(415) 482-3217
Residential treatment facility for recovering mothers and their infants.

UCLA Infant and Family Services Project
U.C.L.A. Department of Pediatrics
100 Veterans Avenue, Rm. 23-10 Rehab.
Los Angeles, CA 90024-1797
(213) 825-9527
Provides child assessment and parent education for medically fragile children with substance exposure, age newborn to two years.

Scott Newman Center
6255 Sunset Boulevard, Suite 1906
Los Angeles, CA 90028
(800)783-6396
Information about services available to drug involved families.

District of Columbia

Howard Univ.Child Development Center
525 Bryant Street N.W.
Washington, DC 20059
(202) 806-6973
Developmental assessment and medical treatment for children with substance exposure.

Florida

Operation PAR (Parental Awareness and Responsibility)
13800 66th Street
North Largo, FL 34641
(813) 538-7244
Residential treatment services for children with substance exposure and their mothers.

Partnerships to Empower Parents
11025 S.W. 84th Street, Cottage 11
Miami, FL 33173
(305) 271-2211
Assists drug-affected families in assessing and developing support networks.

Georgia

Georgia Addiction, Pregnancy and Parenting Project
1256 Briarcliff Road N.E.
Suite 324 West
Atlanta, GA 30306
(404) 894-8288
Treatment/intervention program for pregnant women with substance abuse problems and their infants.

PEBBLES (Perinatally Exposed Babies: Building Linkages and Expertise)
Child Welfare Institute
1365 Peachtree Street, Suite 700
Atlanta, GA 30309
(404) 876-1934
Increases the capacity of foster and adoptive families to care for children with drug exposure and/or HIV through training and support; provides information concerning local resources; provides multidisciplinary team support.

Project Prevent
Grady Memorial Hospital
100 Edgewood Avenue N.E., Rm. 812
Atlanta, GA 30335
(404) 616-4924
Program to lessen the incidence of abandonment of infants with drug exposure and HIV, through primary and secondary prevention.

Illinois

Perinatal Center for Chemical Dependence
680 North Lakeshore Drive, Suite 824
Chicago, IL 60611
(312) 908-0867
Treatment and research center serving chemically dependent women and their children.

Maryland

Family Centered Services for Children with AIDS, HIV Infection or Drug Exposure
Maryland Dept. of Human Services
311 W. Saratoga Street
Baltimore, MD 21201
(301) 333-0212
Provides a transagency case management system with comprehensive services and recruitment and training of foster/adoptive parents.

Massachusetts

The Kinship Project
1800 Columbus Avenue
Roxbury, MA 02119
(617) 442-7442
Model demonstration project provides national training on the implementation of coordinated service models for children with substance exposure and their families.

Nevada

Resource Development and Coordination Project for Abandoned/At-Risk Infants and Young Children
2527 North Carson Street
Carson City, NV 89710
(702) 687-4874
Provides home-based services to infants, young children and their families who are drug or HIV affected.

New Jersey

Transitional Residence and Multi-Purpose Resource Center for Boarder Babies and Their Families
100 Hamilton Plaza
Patterson, NJ 07505
(201) 977-4000
Transitional residence and other supportive services for Hudson County residents whose children are in "boarder baby" status in county hospitals.

New Mexico

Los Pasos
Ambulatory Care Center, Pediatrics
University of New Mexico Medical School
Albuquerque, NM 87131-5311
(505)272-6843
A multiagency case management project. Enhances family permanency for infants with drug exposure, using comprehensive medical and developmental services for high-risk infants and their families.

New York

Comprehensive Services to Drug and HIV Exposed Children and Families
Children's Hospital PACT Program
125 Hodge Street
Buffalo, NY 14222
(716) 878-7908
Provides outreach support services to pregnant women at high risk for HIV/AIDS, outpatient medical and multidisciplinary support services.

Special Prenatal Program and AIDS Initiative Programs
Harlem Hospital
Perinatal Services
506 Lenox Avenue
New York, NY 10037
(212) 491-1234 (General Information)
(212) 491-4033 (AIDS Programs)
Programs for pregnant and parenting women with substance abuse issues.

Pregnant Addicts and Addicted Mothers Program Center for Comprehensive Health Practice
New York Medical College
1900 2nd Avenue, 12th Floor
New York, NY 10029
(212) 360-7781
Programs for pregnant and parenting women with substance abuse issues.

Pennsylvania

Family Center
Thomas Jefferson Hospital
111 South Walnut Street, Suite 6015
Philadelphia, PA 19107
(215) 928-8577
Treatment program for chemically dependent women and their children.

South Carolina

Working Together
Volunteers of America of the Carolinas
2218 Devine Street
P.O. Box 1447
Columbia, SC 29202-1447
Multidisciplinary teams provide home-based treatment, support and education for drug-involved families.

Tennessee

Great Starts: Mother-Infant Assistance Program
Child and Family Services
114 Damaron
Knoxville, TN 37917
(615) 524-7483
Provides housing and support services for infants with substance exposure and their mothers; recruits and trains foster families to work with at-risk children.

Texas

Model Project for Prevention of Abandoned Children in Texas (MPPACT)
Texas Department of Human Services
P.O. Box 149030
Austin, TX 78714-9030
(512) 450-4966
Provides preventive services to families and rehabilitative services to children with substance exposure.

Washington

Childhaven
Drug Affected Infant Program
4648 Viburnum Court South, Unit 500
Seattle, WA 98122
(206) 723-7442
FAX (206) 723-1735
Provides preventive services to families and rehabilitative services to children with substance exposure.

Appendix E

Further Reading

Fetal Alcohol Syndrome

Dorris, Michael. 1990. *The Broken Cord.* New York: Harper Perennial.

Learning Styles

Guild, Pat and Louise McKinney. n.d. *Using Learning Styles to Help Students Be Successful: A Synthesis of a Study of the Learning Styles of Low Achievers in Seattle Public Schools 1989-1990.* Seattle: Pat Guild Associates.

Slavin, Robert, Nancy Karweit and Nancy Madden. 1989. *Effective Programs for Students at Risk.* Needham Heights, MA: Allyn and Bacon.

Tobias, Cindy and Pat Guild. 1986. *No Sweat! How to Use Your Learning Style to Be a Better Student.* Seattle: The Teaching Advisory.

National Association of Secondary School Principals. 1982. *Student Learning Styles and Brain Behavior.* Reston, VA.

Guidelines for Preschool Programs for At-Risk Children

Los Angeles Unified School District. 1989. *Today's Challenge: Teaching Strategies for Working with Young Children Prenatally Exposed to Drugs/Alcohol.* Los Angeles: Division of Special Education: Prenatally Exposed to Drugs (PED) Program.

Florida Department of Education. 1989. *Cocaine Babies: Florida's Substance Exposed Youth.* Tallahassee: Florida Department of Education, Office of Policy Research and Improvement.

Discussing HIV with Young Children

Quackenbush, Marcia and Sylvia Villarreal. 1988. *Does AIDS Hurt? Educating Young Children About AIDS.* Santa Cruz, CA: ETR Associates

Discussing Cultural and Other Differences with Young Children

Matiella, Ana Consuelo. 1991. *Positively Different: Creating a Bias-Free Environment for Young Children.* Santa Cruz, CA: ETR Associates

Drug Prevention with Young Children

Evans, Gracie and Doris Sanford. 1987. *I Can Say No: A Child's Book About Drug Abuse,* Portland: Multnomah Press.

Schwartz, Linda. 1991. *What Would You Do: A Child Survival Guide,* Santa Barbara: The Learning Works. (Available from Knowledge Industries, 105 Smith Street, Brooklyn, NY 11201.)

References

Ainsworth, M.D.S. 1973. *The development of infant-mother attachment.* In *Review of Child Development Research,* vol. 3, eds. B.M. Caldwell and H.N. Ricciuti. Chicago: University of Chicago Press.

Ainsworth, M.D.S., M. Behar, E. Waters and S. Wall. 1978. *Patterns of attachment behavior in the strange situation and at home.* Hillsdale, NJ: Lawrence Erlbaum.

Barry, E.M. and L. Yu. 1991. Punishing pregnant drug dependent women: The myths about incarceration. *Clearinghouse for Drug-Exposed Children Newsletter* 2 (1): 3.

Beggs, M. 1987. *Drug-exposed babies in the San Francisco Bay area.* San Francisco: Zellerbach Family Fund.

Besharov, D.J. 1990. Crack and kids. *Society.* July/August 1990: 25-26.

Blum, K. 1984. *Handbook of abusable drugs.* New York: Gardner Press, Inc.

Chasnoff, I.J. 1989. Drug use and women: Establishing a standard of care. *Annals of the New York Academy of Science* 562: 208-210.

Chasnoff, I.J., H. Landress and M. Barett. 1990. The prevalence of illicit-drug or alcohol use during pregnancy and discrepancies in mandatory reporting in Pinellas County, Florida. *New England Journal of Medicine* 332: 1202-1206.

Chavkin W. and S.R. Kandall. 1990. Between a "rock" and a hard place: Perinatal drug abuse. *Pediatrics* 85 (2): 223-225.

Dixon, S.D., K. Bresnahan and B. Zuckerman. 1990. Cocaine babies: Meeting the challenge of management. *Contemporary Pediatrics* 7 (6): 70.

Dubowitz, H. 1989. Prevention of child maltreatment: What is known. *Pediatrics* 83 (4): 570-577.

Dwyer, T., A.L. Ponsonby, N.M. Newman and L.E. Gibbons. 1991. Prospective cohort study of prone sleeping position and sudden infant death syndrome. *Lancet* 337: 1244-1247.

Florida Department of Education. 1989. *Cocaine babies: Florida's substance exposed youth.* Tallahassee, FL: Prevention Center, Department of Education, Office of Policy Research and Improvement.

Guild, P. and L. McKinney. n.d. *Using learning styles to help students be successful: A synthesis of a study of the learning styles of low achievers in Seattle public schools, 1989-1990.* Seattle: Pat Guild Associates.

Holden, C. 1989. Street-wise crack research. *Science.* 246: 1376-1381

Howard, J., C. Rodning and V. Kropenske. 1989. The development of young children of substance-abusing parents: Insights from seven years of intervention and research. *Zero to Three* 9 (5): 8-12.

Jackson, S. Crack babies are here! Can you help them learn? *CTA Action* 29 (3): 11.

Kronstadt, D. 1989. *Pregnancy and cocaine addiction: An overview of impact and treatment.* San Francisco: Far West Laboratory for Educational Research and Development.

Los Angeles Unified School District. 1989. *Today's challenge: Teaching strategies for working with young children prenatally exposed to drugs/alcohol.* Los Angeles: Division of Special Education: Prenatally Exposed to Drugs (PED) Program.

Maisto, S.A., M. Galizio and G.J. Connors. 1991. *Drug Use and Misuse.* Fort Worth, TX: Holt, Rinehart and Winston, Inc.

McNulty, M. 1990. Pregnancy police: Implications of criminalizing fetal abuse. *Youth Law News, Special Issue,* 1990: 33-36.

Miller, G. 1989. Addicted infants and their mothers. *Zero to Three* 9 (5): 20-23. (Based on report of the Select Committee on Children, Youth and Families, U.S. House of Representatives.)

National Association of Secondary School Principals. 1982. *Student learning styles and brain behavior.* Reston, VA.

Rosenthal, R. and L. Jacobsen. 1989. *Pygmalion in the classroom: Teacher expectations and pupils' intellectual development.* New York: Irvington.

Schuckit, M.A. *Drug and alcohol abuse: A clinical guide to diagnosis and treatment.* 3d ed. New York: Plenum Medical Book Company.

Slavin, R., N. Karweit, and N. Madden. 1989. *Effective programs for students at risk.* Needham Heights, MA: Allyn and Bacon.

Sokal-Gutierrez, K., H. Vaughn-Edmonds and S.F. Villarreal. In press. *Health care services for children and their families.* In *UC Berkeley Study of Services for Drug- and AIDS-Affected Families,* ed. R. Barth. New York: The Guilford Press.

Tobias, C. and P. Guild. 1986. *No sweat! How to use your learning style to be a better student.* Seattle: The Teaching Advisory.

Udell, B. 1989. Crack Cocaine. *Special Currents: Cocaine Babies.* Columbus, OH: Ross Laboratories.

Young, P. 1988. *Drugs and pregnancy.* Bryn Mawr, PA: Chelsea House Educational Talking Books.

Glossary

active learner—A person who "learns by doing" (see **kinesthetic learner**).

addiction—Physical or psychological dependence on a substance. Overwhelming involvement with acquiring and using a substance; inability to stop using; tendency to start using again after periods of abstinence.

at-risk—Describes children who, for a variety of reasons, have an increased likelihood of school failure, physical illness or family dysfunction. Includes children with prenatal drug or alcohol exposure, children from drug- or alcohol-involved families, children with chronic or severe medical conditions, children who are abused, children in poverty and others.

amphetamine—A type of central nervous system stimulant.

analytic learner—Part to whole learner. Infers the larger concept by coordinating various separate pieces of information or data.

auditory learner—A person who learns by hearing things. Describes information and experience in auditory terms.

bonding—In infants and young children, the ability to make a deep, personal connection with a primary caregiver.

central nervous system—The brain and spinal cord.

chemical dependency—A psychological or physical dependence on a substance. (See **addiction** and **dependence**.)

chemically exposed—In this context, a child who has experienced prenatal exposure to substances, including alcohol or illicit drugs, through the mother's use during pregnancy.

Child Protective Services—An agency authorized by county, state and federal laws to receive reports of known or suspected child abuse or neglect, assess families and children where abuse is known or suspected to have occurred, and make recommendations concerning custody of children or rehabilitation of parents.

cognition—Thinking.

cognitive development—The process through which children learn to think, to incorporate information into their experience, and to communicate this knowledge to others.

CNS—See **central nervous system.**

CPS—See **Child Protective Services.**

deficit—Area of weakness.

dependence—Reliance on use of a substance. In *psychological* dependence, which is possible with all drugs, the user needs to use the substance of choice to achieve a state of well-being. In *physical* dependence, which is possible with some drugs, the body has adapted to use of a substance and will experience symptoms of withdrawal if use is stopped.

developmental assessment—Evaluation of a child's intellectual, academic and linguistic status, and how a particular child's status compares to expected levels of development.

developmental milestones—Behaviors and capabilities used to measure a child's developmental progress when compared with a group of children of the same age. A child may achieve a milestone earlier, comparably or more slowly than his or her peers.

drug- and alcohol-involved families—Families in which a parent, child or other member is dependent on drugs or alcohol. Much of the family's focus will center on drug- and alcohol-related issues.

dual diagnosis—A situation in which an individual has a psychiatric diagnosis as well as a chemical dependency.

early intervention—Taking active steps early in a child's life or school career, or at a point where signs or symptoms of distress are new and minimal, to prevent progression to more serious problems.

educational remediation—Therapeutic educational approach tailored to an individual child's learning needs.

failure to thrive—A medical condition characterized by poor weight, height or head growth in an infant or young child.

FAS—See **Fetal Alcohol Syndrome.**

false negative—In toxicology screens, test shows negative results when the person actually has used substance.

false positive—In toxicology screens, test shows positive results when the person actually has not used substance.

Fetal Alcohol Effect—A diagnosis given to a child who shows signs and symptoms of prenatal exposure to alcohol of lesser degree than a child diagnosed with Fetal Alcohol Syndrome.

Fetal Alcohol Syndrome—A syndrome caused by prenatal exposure to alcohol through maternal use. Characterized by small head size, mental retardation, heart or other organ defects, and facial features including small eyes, drooping eyelids, flat midface, and a simple philtrum (underdevelopment or absence of the indentation in the upper lip).

fine motor coordination—Coordination of small or detailed motor (movement) tasks, such as turning pages of a book, holding a glass of juice, drawing, fastening buttons.

global learner—Whole to part learner. Learns best by starting with a whole concept, then breaking it down into component parts.

gross motor coordination—Coordination of large motor (movement) behaviors, such as crawling, walking, running, jumping, carrying, skipping.

hyperreflexia—Overactive reflexes. Reflexes respond easily to stimuli.

hypertonic—A state of muscle stiffness, tightness.

IEP—See **Individualized Educational Program.**

Individualized Educational Program—Public Law 94-142, a federal law, requires that students identified as having special educational needs be accommodated by the school system. When necessary, a meeting is convened of specialists who will evaluate the child's academic and cognitive status. If appropriate, an Individualized Educational Program will be established to provide for the child's educational needs in the least restrictive setting. For example, a child should not be placed in a complete special education program if a tutor is sufficient to meet the child's needs.

information processing—The flow of information in and out of memory; how the mind transforms information to make it usable.

injection drug user—An individual who injects drugs under the skin, into the veins or into the muscles. Preferred to the term "intravenous drug user," or "IVDU," which technically refers only to an individual who injects drugs directly into a vein.

irritability—In the context of pediatric health, a child who is fussy, ill-tempered, hard to sooth and calm.

kinesthetic learner—A person who "learns by doing," by engaging actively in the learning process through movement, touching, feeling.

learning style—The manner in which an individual processes information.

maternal substance use/abuse—Use or abuse of drugs or alcohol by a woman during pregnancy.

milestones —See **developmental milestones.**

negative toxicology screen—See **toxicology screen.**

neurologic—Relating to the nervous system. Especially, a symptom or sign manifesting problems or illness of the nervous system (e.g., a seizure).

neurologist—A physician specializing in disorders of the nervous system.

nystagmus—Involuntary, rapid movement of the eyes from side to side.

overstimulated—In an educational or developmental context, the state of being overwhelmed by sensory input. There is too much to see, hear, smell, feel to be able to separate out the sensations, concentrate on a task, feel secure, and so forth.

perinatal—The period of time in a pregnancy from twelve weeks before delivery, extending to one month after birth.

placental abruption—The shearing or tearing off of the placenta from the uterine wall.

polydrug exposure—Prenatal exposure to multiple substances; for example, if a pregnant woman uses crack cocaine, alcohol and marijuana over the course of her pregnancy, her fetus experiences polydrug exposure. This is a common occurrence.

positive toxicology screen—See **toxicology screen.**

precipitous delivery—A medical condition of pregnancy involving sudden, uncontrolled delivery of the child.

prematurity—A birth before forty weeks gestation.

prenatal—Before birth. The period from the point of conception up to the point of delivery.

prenatal chemical exposure—Fetal exposure to drugs or alcohol through maternal use.

prevention—The avoidance of distress, dysfunction or illness. The emphasis of prevention efforts will vary from setting to setting: medical prevention seeks to avoid illness and injury through behavioral change or reduction of events that can lead to harm; prevention in the educational setting seeks to enhance school success and avoid school failure and drop-out; drug prevention seeks to prevent the abuse of substances.

recovery—A lifelong process supporting abstinence from recreational drugs and alcohol. Involves changes in social, physical and psychological functioning, and often has a spiritual component. This is the philosophy of 12-step programs such as Alcoholics Anonymous. See also **treatment.**

remediation—See **educational remediation.**

seizures—A disturbance of brain function that may result in a number of different outcomes, including loss of consciousness, twitching of muscles, jerkiness in arms and legs, or feeling like one is in a dream.

SIDS—See **Sudden Infant Death Syndrome.**

substance use—Use of drugs and/or alcohol. Substance "use" includes non-pathological or non-dependent use of a substance.

substance abuse—Use of drugs and/or alcohol in a way that presents a danger to oneself or others. Includes, but is not limited to, individuals with chemical dependency.

Sudden Infant Death Syndrome—The sudden and unexpected death of an apparently healthy infant, usually between the ages of three weeks and five months, with no cause found on autopsy.

tachycardia—Faster than normal heart rate. The normal heart rate varies by age, with children having faster heartbeats than adults.

toxicity—A state in which an individual using a substance has ingested a quantity great enough to cause a compromise in vital signs. Often life threatening. Same as **overdose.**

toxicology screen—A test run on samples of urine or blood to determine whether or not an individual has recently used drugs or alcohol. Newborn toxicology screens, performed on newborn urine or blood, indicate whether the mother has recently used drugs or alcohol. A *positive* toxicology screen indicates evidence of substance use was found. A *negative* toxicology screen indicates no evidence of substance use was found.

treatment—In chemical dependency, a program to assist an individual end a dependency on a particular substance. Treatment approaches are not necessarily abstinence programs. For example, a person in a methadone maintenance program is being treated for heroin addiction by receiving another drug, methadone.

visual learner—A person who learns by seeing things. Describes information and experience in visual terms.

well-baby visit—A regularly scheduled visit with a medical provider to evaluate a child's development and health status. Not specifically related to an illness or symptom. Immunizations may be given or laboratory tests obtained at such visits. Prevention is emphasized.

withdrawal—Physical or psychological symptoms resulting from decreasing or ending use of a substance when a person is dependent on the substance. Often, withdrawal symptoms oppose the effects of the substance itself—a person withdrawing from stimulants will be slowed down and depressed, and a person withdrawing from depressants will be agitated and anxious. Withdrawal from some substances can be life threatening and may require close medical supervision.

Index

Additional information may be found in the appendixes, which were not included in this index.

About the Authors

Sylvia Fernandez Villarreal, MD, received her medical degree from Stanford University in 1977. She served her pediatric residency and was also chief resident at the University of Colorado, Denver, and was a member of the medical school faculty there from 1981 to 1984. She was a Robert Wood Johnson Scholar from 1984 to 1986, where her research looked at Hispanic health and national survey data on Mexican-American sexual maturation. She is currently Assistant Clinical Professor of Pediatrics, University of California, San Francisco, and is also Director of Early Childhood Services at San Francisco General Hospital. She is director of the Kempe High Risk Clinic, which serves teen mothers and their children, infants with chemical exposure and their mothers, and children who fail to thrive. Her current clinical research is in Latina teen pregnancy and chemical addiction in mothers and children.

Lora-Ellen McKinney, PhD, is Assistant Clinical Professor in the Division of Behavioral and Developmental Pediatrics at the University of California, San Francisco, and is an associate director of training for the Clinical Psychology Training Faculty at Langley Porter Psychiatric Institute at UCSF. She earned her PhD in clinical psychology from the University of Washington in Seattle. She presently serves as the director of the Learning Evaluation Program in the Division of Behavioral and Developmental Pediatrics, a program designed to assess and treat children with neurobehavioral and learning problems. Her primary research interest is in the area of developmental outcomes of children at risk for developmental disorders. Dr. McKinney is the director of the Clearinghouse for Drug Exposed Children at UCSF, a community service that provides resource and referral information to caregivers and providers working with children with drug exposure.

Marcia Quackenbush, MS, MFCC, has been writing on children's health issues since 1979. She has a master's degree in counseling from San Francisco State University, and a California license in Marriage, Family and Child Counseling. Her early clinical emphasis was in child and family mental health, and she has worked in the AIDS/HIV field since 1984, offering direct service to persons with HIV and professional training to providers. She is currently Coordinator of Special Projects with the AIDS Health Project, a program of the University of California, San Francisco. Ms. Quackenbush has collaborated on several books on AIDS/HIV education, including *Teaching AIDS, The AIDS Challenge* and *Does AIDS Hurt? Educating Young Children About AIDS* (all published by ETR Associates). She has a private practice in psychotherapy and is also an illustrator and photographer.

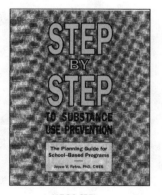

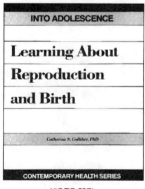

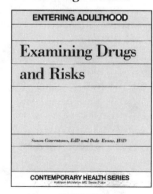